Reinventing the Sale

Maximise your business potential

Reinventing the Sale

Published in the UK

Copyright © 2014 John Rees

All rights reserved.

No part of this work may be reproduced without the permission of the copyright owner.

ISBN: 978-1502960023

TABLE OF CONTENTS

4	**Foreword**
	The 5 principles of success
	Stumbling blocks
14	**Section one - Messages**
	Message essentials
	Headlines
	Message stack
	Worksheet
74	**Section two - Strategy**
	Assessing potential
	Creating the plan
	Worksheet
	Executing the plan
162	**Section three - Relationships**
	Selling defined
	Top performers
	Buying and selling
	Navigator sales process
	Presenting your ideas
	Worksheet
235	**About me**

FOREWORD

Every business owner knows how hard it is to achieve sales success. But being good at selling is only part of the equation. There are other skills you must master to maximise your business potential.

> I've been involved in sales and marketing for more than 35 years. During this time I've been a salesperson, manager and director and I've generated hundreds of millions of dollars worth of product and service sales.
>
> I've worked with global corporations you've heard of, and some small fast growth companies you haven't. Some were wildly successful but others failed. So I've seen both sides of the success equation, and it taught me a lot about what works and what doesn't.
>
> I've used this experience to identify the 5 Principles of Success that drives strong and sustainable growth.
>
> **More on that later.**

Although I've spent most of my life working in the Information Technology sector, the lessons I've learned apply to any business, in any sector.

The IT industry is ultra-competitive, fast moving and exciting. But there's a tendency to over-complicate things and confuse with too much information and jargon.

It doesn't have to be like this though.

I've always made it as easy as possible for buyers to understand what I can do, and why I'm different. I've developed this thinking, and created 'Reinventing the Sale' to help any business can use to transform the way it sells.

One of the biggest barriers to success is complexity. That's why Reinventing the Sale is designed to help you simplify and improve everything you do.

Reinventing the Sale isn't theory though. It's based on years of experience that has enabled me to succeed, and it can do exactly the same for you.

If you'd like to learn more or contact me directly, please visit www.reinventingthesale.com.

THE 5 PRINCIPLES OF SUCCESS

To achieve consistent and repeatable success you must do the following, which I call the 5 principles of success.

I know this is quite a list and it comprises skills many people don't posses. That may be true now, but that's where Reinventing the Sale comes in.

It will help you to develop the skills, strategies and actions you'll need to drive and sustain the strong sales growth that your business needs.

Reinventing the Sale has 3 sections (Messages, Strategy and Relationships) that covers all 5 principles of success. It will teach you simple, powerful and proven ideas and skills that will help you to achieve results you want.

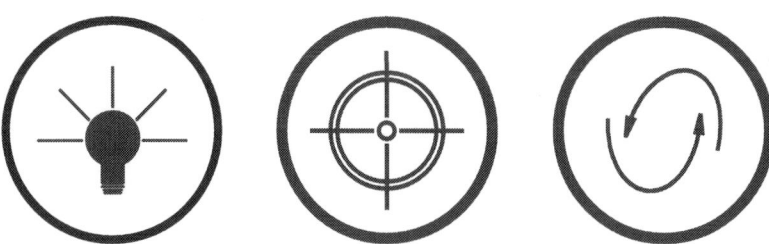

Reinventing the Sale will teach you how to;

- Create powerful messages to describe your difference;
- Develop the right strategy to build an audience;
- Select the best channels to sell through;
- Generate high quality sales enquiries;
- Communicate in a way that attracts attention;
- Use the right sales skills to win business;
- Develop long-term mutually profitable relationships;

- Build a 'fan base' who will buy again and refer others to you;

- Improve everything you do to stay ahead of the competition.

WHO IS THE BOOK FOR?

Anyone who has a product, service or idea to sell will benefit from reading Reinventing the Sale.

No previous sales or marketing experience is needed, because it's been specifically written to be easy to understand.

The aim is to simplify and demystify the whole process of sales and marketing and enable even complete novices to understand what it takes to succeed.

The only thing you will need is a desire to learn, and a commitment to take action.

You could be the founder of a startup with great ideas but limited sales experience.

You will learn the skills you need to help your business accelerate.

You could be a manager, director or owner of an established business who wants to do better.

You will learn how to look at your business differently. I will give you a structure to implement world-class ideas and processes that will propel your business forward.

You could be a marketing person who needs to produce more compelling content.

You will learn how to build a healthy supply of sales opportunity. I will give you the tools you need to create a compelling sales story and messages that attract attention and arouse interest.

You could be a salesperson who wants to hit your target and make more money.

You will learn how to use world-class sales skills to improve your performance, and close more business.

You may be a student or an educator.

You will learn about the practical experiences and the harsh facts of life in a competitive business environment.

Whoever you are, I know you'll get some value by reading on!

But before we go any further, let's just consider some of the typical barriers to success that I've seen.

These will help you to understand why I started to think about success in a more holistic way.

STUMBLING BLOCKS

We all know that success is often illusive. Life seems to throw things in our way to stop us achieving what we feel we deserve, or desperately desire.

Over the years I've worked with many businesses across different sectors, and the following are comments I've heard many times;

"We don't have enough prospects to sell to."

"Sales performance is patchy and we struggle to meet our targets."

"Sales just take too long to close."

"We seem to be losing more sales than we win."

"We lose sales we should really be winning."

Because these comments are all related to sales, it seems reasonable to blame your sales team for being a bunch of underachieving time-wasting losers right? That is true in some cases, but not always! Let's look more closely.

"We don't have enough prospects to sell to."

Salespeople generally hate making cold calls, so you could assume this is a sales problem.

There are other possible issues though, such as a poorly executed marketing strategy, a website that doesn't work or messages that don't attract attention, arouse interest and inspire a buyer to learn more.

Perhaps you are also trying to sell to the wrong people! Strange as it seems this does happen. Unless you clearly define your target buyers, and understand why they would be receptive to your messages, you will get patchy results.

Your website should be a magnet that generates enquiries. If it's not, it could be down to poor design and weak uninspiring content.

You may also have an unstructured approach to generating sales leads, and only worry about creating opportunities when you don't have any.

This is very common, as people only focus on closing business they can see. When that's out of the way, the panic sets in and they try to 'drum up' interest in a hurry. The results are not usually good.

"Sales just take too long to close."

This could be because your salespeople are not very good, in which case you should either train or replace them.

But sales performance isn't always the cause. A big factor could be that you don't work in a structured way. You may have a poor or non-existent sales process. This means you often don't qualify opportunities very well, and chase any and every 'opportunity' even where the chances of success are pretty slim.

Perhaps you don't regularly review sales strategies and coach salespeople to focus on where they can win?

All these things result in poor sales productivity, which is why sales can take too long to close.

"We seem to lose sales we should be winning."

This could be a sales performance issue, but it could also be that your product or service just isn't competitive.

There are others that are better, faster, cheaper, easier to use and have a stronger, more compelling value proposition. They just have a better fit for the buyer than you do, and they put their message across in a more clear, concise and compelling way.

In short, you're being outsold by competitors with a better product.

Perhaps your sales messages are feature rich, benefit light and generally uninspiring. Your unique selling proposition isn't really that unique.

I'm sure you get the point, that in any of these situations there is an effect (sluggish growth) but potentially many causes.

However, it is easy to see why underachievement is seen as a sales performance problem. And that's why people focus purely on one aspect, such as lead generation or improving their sales process, if they even have one!

The problem is that these are isolated initiatives that can make some improvements, but they don't address the underlying issues. Sustainable success requires more than an isolated one dimensional isolated fix. A broader approach is needed, and that's exactly why I developed Reinventing the Sale.

SECTION ONE
Messages

HOW TO MAKE YOUR BRIGHT IDEAS SHINE

You start a business because you have a great business idea, product or service. But that's not always enough to succeed, because unless you attract attention it'll be a well kept secret. And you'll probably go out of business!

> Today there's so much competition for attention. The people you are trying to reach are already being bombarded with messages from many different sources. There's a relentless battle being waged to make your audience aware of the latest, and greatest idea they just can't live without!
>
> This makes it harder than ever to break through, which is why it's so important to grab your audience's attention and motivate them to buy from you.
>
> The way you attract attention is through messages that achieve results every time. And that's what I'll cover in this section.

I'll talk about the most important characteristics any message must have.

I'll describe what headlines are, and why they are so important.

And I'll introduce you to a unique model I've developed to make it easier than ever to create stunning and effective messages. It's called Message Stack.

There's also a worksheet you can use to create your own messages and put the ideas into immediate use.

So let's get started!

 ## MESSAGE ESSENTIALS

The most important thing you must understand to create powerful messages, is that they must be clear, concise and compelling.

It's pretty simple really. The easier you make it for someone to understand, and be enthusiastic about your idea, the more successful you'll be.

This may seem blindingly obvious and it is. But so many people overcomplicate things, and that's why their messages don't work very well.

So let's look at what clear, concise and compelling actually means;

> Clear - very easy to understand;

> Concise - as short and detailed as possible;

> Compelling - grabs attention and motivates action.

Before I get into the specifics of creating 'C3' messages, I want to talk about simplicity.

As I said earlier, simplicity really is the essence of effective communication.

This has been acknowledged throughout history by some of the greatest thinkers and artists.

Leonardo Da Vinci knew the value of simplicity. And his *"simplicity is the ultimate sophistication"* quotation is well know.

Chinese philosopher Confucius also saw the value of simplicity by saying *" Life is really simple, but we insist on making it complicated."* I couldn't agree more!

Apple's entire product and service focus is on simplicity, and that's why it takes things out of its products to make them as easy to use as possible. As the late Steve Jobs said;

> "Simple can be harder than complex: you have to work hard to get your thinking clean to make it simple. But once you get there, you can move mountains."

Nest is another company that's taken a fresh look at boring things like thermostats and smoke alarms. Their designs are simple and elegant. And if you're like me, and you've struggled to understand your heating system, Nest solves the problem beautifully.

The way you achieve simplicity in a message is to get to the absolute core by using as few words as possible. This means eliminating those 'filler' words that don't actually mean anything. They just bloat your story and make it more long-winded and confusing than it needs to be.

The best way to achieve simplicity in a message is to edit ruthlessly. This obviously takes time and patience, but it's worth the effort to get the best result.

As well as padding, the other killers are jargon, buzzwords and slang. These are unfortunately in common use today, but they complicate messages and confuse people.

I hate them because they sound pretentious and empty.

Here's what I mean;

"Let's drill down on that" … analyse

"That's on my radar" … I'm aware of it

"Let's touch base" …make contact

"It's a real paradigm shift" … new

"We should circle back" … catch up later

"I'm reaching out to you" … contacting

"Let's take that one offline" … later

"We should arrange some quality face time" … let's meet

So my best advice is to never use words and phrases that don't mean anything. Or where possible, always use the simplest words to get your point across.

How to make your message clear

You can achieve clarity with a message through the language you use, and the way you use it.

David Ogilvy is a legendary advertising man and master communicator, and he said you must use language your audience will easily understand. This is another obvious statement that many people ignore.

Whether you sell professional services to Fortune 500 corporations, or skateboards to people under 25, you must use language they will respond to.

If you're describing some technical or scientific concept, you'll obviously need to use appropriate language to describe it. Although this may not be understood by the uninitiated, you should try to make even the complicated, relatively easy to understand.

If you work in different geographic regions you should also be aware of any linguistic and cultural issues, and create messages that are acceptable and don't cause unintended offence.

The style of communication will also have an impact on how your messages look and sound. Some people use a 'third person' style which is formal, for example;

> *"David Green is a marketing and sales professional. He has worked with many different organisations around the world."*

This is probably fine in some situations but not in others. If someone else is talking about you in a biographical way, or if this is on a company website it can work well.

But if you're writing about yourself it just doesn't sound right. Some people may use it to try to build an image that their business is bigger than it is. Or perhaps they think that's the way it should be.

A 'first person' tone is much more informal because it reads and sounds like a personal conversation between you (David Green) and the listener or reader. It's conversational and altogether warmer and more friendly.

> "Hello, I'm David Green and I'm a marketing and sales professional …"

So the best way to create a clear message is to do these 5 things;

1. Keep it simple;

2. Cut the padding;

3. Eliminate jargon;

4. Use the right language;

5. Personalise your message.

How to make messages concise

I've already talked about the need to cut to the core, and that's one very important way to make your message concise.

The other way is to use words that attract attention. Words that have an impact. Words that convey a lot of meaning. Words that paint a powerful mental picture.

Power words

These are words that can dramatise and emphasise. When they are used in the right context, they can help your message seem more compelling and potent.

But be careful how you use them, or they can backfire and appear untruthful.

In fact, when they are used in the wrong context or used too frequently, they become buzzwords.

Here are some power words;

Accelerate	Guaranteed	Soaring
Amazing	Improved	Spectacular
Authentic	Innovative	Staggering
Bargain	Inspirational	Stimulate
Boost	Jubilant	Stunning
Benefit	Luxurious	Surge
Breathtaking	Magnificent	Tantalising
Compelling	Multiply	Unconditional
Delight	Powerful	Unique
Efficient	Profitable	Uplifting
Empower	Proven	Value
Enhance	Quadruple	Wonderful
Exciting	Sensational	You
Explode	Simplify	
Free	Skyrocket	

Being concise is also about saying what you mean and meaning what you say.

If you lie to people and don't keep your sales promises, they will lose faith in you and go elsewhere. That's why honesty will always win you more fans in the long run.

Of course you should be upbeat and very positive about what you do. But be careful. Describing something as unique, stunning or guaranteed is fine, if that's true. But don't make wild and outrageous claims you can't support. People will usually see through this and you'll lose their trust. And when you do, you'll also lose their business.

Also avoid using 'weasel words'. These are vague and ambiguous statements that are designed to attract attention, but they are misleading. They make a promise that's usually not kept and this destroys trust. This is a very bad idea, because unless people trust you, they generally won't do business with you.

> *"Limited time sale, up to 50% off."*

This is a good example of how weasel words are used. It's the 'up to' bit that's the get out.

Some products will have 50% discount but others will have less. Some will have no discount at all.

If you mean 50% discount on everything, say it.

> *"For one day only, 50% off all our products"*.

So the way you create a concise message is;

1. Cut to the core;

2. Use power words;

3. Tell the truth;

4. Say what you mean;

5. Mean what you say.

If you've done this right, you've attracted attention and created interest with a message that's clear and concise. For it to achieve results, it must also have a strong benefit attached; in other words …

It must be compelling

People buy to solve a problem, satisfy a need or desire. And that's the crux of what makes something compelling.

It's the way it uniquely solves the problem or satisfies a desire, because this is what motivates people to take action.

When these needs and desires are obvious and people recognise them, the task is easy. You just describe what you sell as a solution to the need. But if the audience doesn't know they need what you're selling, you must take a different approach.

You create the desire.

In 1908 Henry Ford introduced something new, the model-T motor car.

There was no demand, just a dream Henry had of changing the world. And making a lot of money along the way!

He didn't run any focus groups or conduct detailed market research. If he had, it would have told him not to bother. It probably would have confirmed what he is believed to have said;

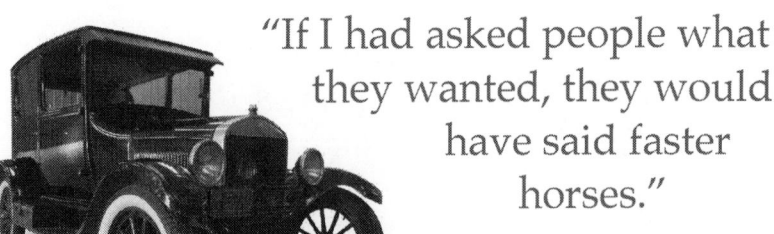

"If I had asked people what they wanted, they would have said faster horses."

Reinventing the Sale

Fast forward 93 years to 2001, when Apple introduced the first generation iPod with the slogan "1,000 songs in your pocket".

No-one knew they needed it. In fact, Sony had the mobile music market sewn up with Walkman CD players and cassettes (remember them?).

The CD players were good, but you had to carry many discs around. There were some solid state MP3 players, but they were difficult to use and upload music to.

So although no-one was screaming for an iPod, there was latent demand for a better way to listen to music on the move. And when Apple showed us a way of replacing the other devices with their new iPod, we just loved it.

Since then iPod iPhone and iPad have become portable entertainment, information and productivity devices that millions of us use every day.

The point of all this is that if people don't know what they want, or even that they need something, you must show them what they are missing!

Making a decision to buy can be very difficult.

In well defined markets with established products and services, buyers generally know what they are looking for. They will probably have evaluated different products against some key criteria such as price, availability, service, product features and value for money.

But when a product is brand new there will be little, if any competition. Buyers will then think about a product differently.

Some may shy away from being early users. Others are keen to buy something new, cool and exciting. These are the 'early adopters' and for them, being first has a certain cache.

In both cases though, you want to make it easy for people by telling them what makes your product different. This is sometimes called a Unique Selling Point. But this term has been so over-used that many people view it with suspicion.

Think about it for a second …

Unique literally means 'being the only one of its kind' or 'unlike anything else' and if you can say that, you really do have a USP.

In reality, finding a true (and provable) USP is very difficult. Some products are anonymous because they have no distinct advantage, they are commodities in a crowded market. They generally compete on lowest price which can work, but it can also put you out of business.

When you think about USP, include everything such as special features, price, value for money, peace of mind, warranty and after-sales service.

Stress the benefits

Being different is obviously important, but only when it has a benefit attached. And as I said earlier, the benefit depends on whether you are satisfying a need or creating one.

So let's now look at how you create a benefit statement. A good way to think about this is to use the F.A.B. formula. This stands for Feature-Advantage-Benefit, and it's a great way to identify the 'real' benefit, because people often get confused here.

Feature is the way something works;

Advantage is what it does better than the alternatives;

Benefit is what that means to the buyer;

For example;

My new car has a hybrid engine
(*Feature*);

Which makes it 45% more fuel efficient than other cars
(*Advantage*);

This means I save more than £1,500 a year on fuel costs
(*Benefit*);

You see, it's easy.

So the way you create a compelling message is to;

1. Satisfy a need or create one;

2. Show why you are different;

3. Deliver real benefits.

When you pull all these things together, you have a clear, concise and compelling message that attracts attention, arouses interest and motivates action.

What you now need is a way of summarising this into as few words as possible. In other words, you need a stunning headline!

And that's what I'll talk about next.

 # HEADLINES

David Ogilvy knew a thing or two about how to write headlines. He is regarded by many people as 'The Father of Advertising.'

In 1962, Time Magazine called him 'the most sought-after wizard in today's advertising industry.' His best-selling book 'Confessions of an Advertising Man' was published more than 40 years ago, but it's still one of the most popular books on advertising today. In it he said;

> "The headline is the most important element in most advertisements. On average, five times as many people read the headline as the body copy."

So a headline is probably the most important message you'll ever write, because its primary purpose is to motivate people to read the rest of your message.

The email subject line that you either read or ignore, is a headline. It tells you what the message is about, and in that split second you decide whether it's worth your time reading or hitting the delete button.

The status update, or post on any social media platform is a headline that either motivates you to read further or move on to something else.

How to create a headline that grabs attention

A headline is a message, so the rules I spoke about earlier apply here as they do for any message. In other words, it must be clear, concise and compelling.

Before we get into the mechanics though, you must also ensure that you incorporate these three things into your headline;

1. Who your audience is;

2. The most important thing they'll be interested in;

3. What will motivate them to take action.

This obviously makes sense because it's the best way of grabbing their attention. After all, people are more interested in the things they care about. And that's more likely to motivate them to take action.

There are 2 proven ways to create a headline;

1. As a summary of your story;

2. From an idea;

As a summary of your story

Here you distill the message into a short version that tells the whole story. You do this by reviewing the story to bring out the key point, and that's your headline. For example;

'Titanic sinks after hitting iceberg'

This was shocking because Titanic was thought to be unsinkable. The seven word headline says it all, the rest of the story provides the detail of how, when and why it may have happened.

'Hitler Dead'

This is another headline that tells the story in two words. If you want to know the full detail you will read on.

From an idea

Let's assume that your business has a unique way of helping people save money on their energy bills. I know, its not very exciting, but it's proof that even the mundane needs to be spiced up! Your headline could look like this;

'Guaranteed to cut energy costs in half'

If you target the right audience they may be interested enough to read more about what you do, and how they can slash their energy bills in half.

But remember that the message must support the headline. That's why sensationalist headlines that attract attention but don't keep the promise, will fail to achieve a result.

Some headlines, especially those you see in the press, use a clever play on words. Some use humour, while others are risky and even downright provocative. They rely on the shock factor to get your attention.

Curiosity also works well, because humans are naturally curious creatures. When you arouse curiosity, create a mystery or have a secret, people will want to know more about it.

I know we live in a politically correct time, but don't be afraid to take a few risks. After all if you're the same as everyone else, you just melt into the background and never get noticed. So be bold, be different, offer a fresh perspective and you will attract attention.

Let's now talk about the different types of headline you can create. Some are more effective than others, so you should experiment to see what works best for you.

Direct

This gets straight to the point with minimal word play. It's almost a command or instruction to do something;

"Call us today to cut your fuel bill in half."

Indirect

This makes the point in a more roundabout way and it also arouses curiosity;

"How would you like to cut you fuel bill in half?"

News

This is an announcement of a new or improved offering;

"A new product that will cut your fuel bill in half - or your money back!"

How to

This offers a promise of valuable information;

"Learn how to cut your fuel bill in half."

Now I've covered the basics, I want to introduce you to a structure that makes it so much easier to develop messages that will attract attention and build an audience you can sell to. This is called Message Stack.

MESSAGE STACK

Message Stack will help you to create clear, concise and compelling message and it has four parts;

1. Inspiring Vision
2. Power Summary
3. Engaging Story
4. Content Library

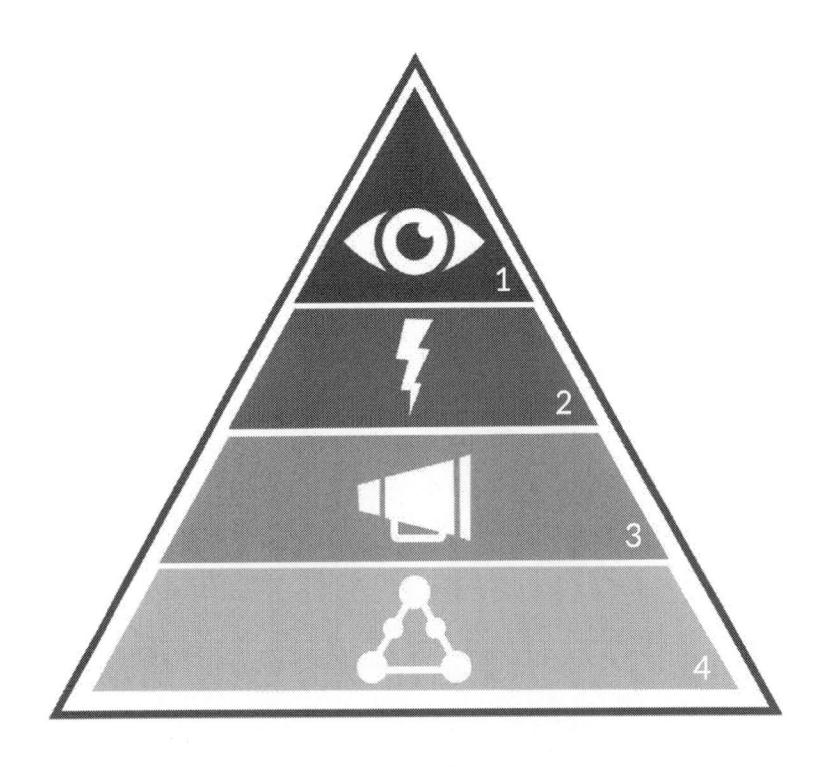

1. Any great message starts with a powerful and evocative headline. And that's a perfect description of an **Inspiring Vision**. It should be a clear concise and compelling description of how you see your future.

2. From this you create a **Power Summary** which is a high level attention grabbing statement of 50 words or less. This is designed to answer the *'what do you do?'* question. Your answer should get the response *'interesting, tell me more'* which gets the conversation started.

3. When it does get going, you tell your **Engaging Story.** This provides more detail, but it's still concise and ideally no more than 300-400 words, or one side of an A4 page.

4. When you have these 3 nailed, you can extend the story to suit many different situations. This is where you build a **Content Library**.

So let's get started and look at how you create an Inspiring Vision

INSPIRING VISION

The dictionary definition of a vision is;

'a mental image of what the future could be like.'

So your Inspiring Vision must describe where you want to be in the future.

"I have a dream ..."

These are 4 words that almost everyone will know. It's part of a speech you may not have read, but I'll bet you know who said it.

Of course it was Martin Luther King Jr, and in this 1963 speech, he set out his vision for what he hoped American society would become.

His speech eventually did change America's attitude towards civil rights. It almost took half a century and unfortunately he didn't live to see it, but it did happen when Barrack Obama was elected the first African-American President in 2009.

Visions are very powerful enablers of change in all walks of life.

This is especially true in business. But rather than being a dream, they should incorporate your core values, beliefs, ethics and ambition. And this should be backed up with action to make it a reality.

Why you need a vision

Before I get into this, I think there are a five key questions we need to consider;

1. How do you operate if you don't have a vision?

2. If you have no defined vision, why do you exist?

3. How do you know what you want to achieve in the future?

4. How do you ensure the world knows what you stand for?

5. What guides your strategy and business activities?

Having no vision is like setting out on a journey with no destination in mind. You may get lost, consume more resources than you need to and have no way of knowing how successful you've been.

Don't think about vision as being a tag line or glib marketing slogan with buzz words or jargon.

Think about it as a statement of why you exist, what you believe in, and what you are striving to achieve.

Vision should be a key driver of your go to market strategy, and an inspiration for your audience, employees and partners. It's also the starting point or headline that drives the development of all your other messages.

That's why it's called Inspiring Vision!

How to create an Inspiring Vision

The basic foundation is the same as for any other message. You probably know by now that means it must be clear, concise and compelling!

Your Inspiring Vision is a simple statement that describes what you aspire to achieve and how this benefits your audience.

To create it does take a bit of thought, and I've developed a simple formula to help you;

1. Purpose - why you exist;

2. Audience - who you want to influence;

3. Values - your beliefs;

4. Ambition - what you want to achieve.

Purpose

Every business must generate sales to succeed.

But if your only motivation and purpose is to make money, that's not very interesting to others. In fact, most people are only interested in themselves, so that's why it's better to explain how you make their life better.

This could be by improving a product or service to make it easier to use, less expensive and generally better in some way. Or you invent something new, which gives the buyer a different and better experience than they currently get.

So what's your story?

Do you know why your business exists and what it's true purpose is?

If you are the founder of your business, you will probably have a very personal story to tell. You can talk about the problem or opportunity you saw, and why you wanted to do something about it.

Audience

Your Inspiring Vision must obviously be relevant and interesting for your audience. So it stands to reason that the better you know what interests and motivates them, the more effective your messages will be.

Define who they are, what they do for a living and even the things they are most interested in.

Some businesses build 'personas' or profiles that includes their age range, income levels, location, educational background, what they will read and even watch on television. How deeply you go into this will depend on what you sell and how you operate.

The key thing here is that when you know what they are interested in, your messages are more likely to succeed. I told you it was simple!

Values

Values are what you regard as important. They define your attitude, the way you behave and ultimately determine how you see the world and do business. They are also key factors that will shape your Inspiring Vision.

If you think that profit is more important than people, you will focus on running your business cost-effectively.

This may mean paying your people as little as possible, and trying to extract maximum value from every customer. You will think and probably act like a low-cost business. You may think this is good practice and it can drive profits, but at what cost? You may alienate customers and have a high staff turnover and low morale. And that will be bad for business in the long run.

If you think that people are your most valuable asset, you'll create the best environment for them to perform in.

If you want to create gorgeous products that people will love, you will have a strong design ethic at the heart of your business.

I'm sure you get the point. The values you have will shape the way you think and operate.

The way you implement these values and behave will develop your reputation. A good reputation generally means that you are highly regarded and trusted. This is great for business as long as it's authentic. If it's not, it'll be very hard to maintain.

'Actions speak louder than words' summarises it nicely, because you can only create a reputation by what you consistently do, rather than by what you say.

And that's even more important in today's online world, where almost everyone is visible.

If you have any online presence, people can generally find out something about you. And unless they've dealt with you before, they'll take what they find as a starting point. So you'd better make sure it's good!

People will post comments about you, offer opinions, criticise or praise you on eBay, Facebook, LinkedIn, Google+ and on many other sites. The sum of these things is what determines your online reputation. And you can make sure it's a fair reflection, by sticking to your principles and doing what you believe is the right thing. In other words, you are true to your values.

Ambition

This is important because it determines what motivates you and it shapes how you work.

So what do you want to achieve? I mean really achieve and not just dream about.

Some people are very clear about this and they can quantify it in ways such as;

- Achieve £20 million in revenues;

- Deliver a 20% profit margin;

- Employ 150 people;

- Have office in London, Paris and New York;

Or it could be;

- Work from home as a full-time designer / writer / mentor (delete as appropriate!)

- Earn £50,000 / £100,000 a year (you decide);

- Work with clients in the (define your space) sector;

- Work 4 days a week;

Unfortunately many people have difficulty with this. They just carry on day in, day out, hoping that something good will happen. But that's not good enough. If you do that you'll never develop. You'll just keep bumping along, paying the bills and probably working harder than you need to.

To make this real and achievable, you must relate it to your purpose. I know this is obvious, but again that's the whole point. Remember, simplicity is best.

Reinventing the Sale

Where do you want to be in 12 months and 3 years from now? This is a hard question to answer, so let's pretend you have a time machine, like Doctor Who.

Note to non-UK readers or non-sci-fi fans: If you've never heard of him, Doctor Who is a fictional TV character and he's a time lord. He travels about in what looks like an old police call box, but it's actually a time machine. It's called Tardis which is short for 'Time and relative dimensions in space'. This could be very useful for many reasons. You could go back and find the winning lottery numbers and a host of other useful things. But as I said, it's fictional, so let's get on with the story!

You can now set your Tardis in motion and travel to the future, say 3 years from now. If you look at your business, what's changed?

- Are you offering the same product or service?
- How many people do you have?
- How many clients do you have?
- Where are they located?
- How have your revenues and profits grown?
- What have you learned since you started?

The reason for looking at it like this, is to think about the future and how you can create it.

Will you need to hire more people, find new partners, secure more investment, develop a new product or service, expand into new premises?

Perhaps your business will be just the same as it is today.

You may have more clients and have improved the quality of your work. Or you are better known and more widely respected for what you do. That's also fine, because ambition isn't always about generating more money, hiring more people or having bigger premises.

There are different measures of what success means. To many people, especially single person businesses, success is all about working on their own terms. Being able to balance a desired level of income with a family, lifestyle or hobby.

So whatever success looks like for you, is absolutely fine. After all, the best businesses are those that are true to their beliefs.

Pulling it all together

I've covered a lot of ground, now it's time to pull it all together to create your Inspiring Vision.

The best way to write it is to use this simple structure;

1. It's not just about you;

2. It should be simple and memorable;

3. It must be realistic and achievable;

1. It's not just about you

As I said earlier, a vision is compelling when it has significance for your audience. Here's a good example;

> 'To be earth's most customer centric company; to build a place where people can come to find and discover anything they might want to buy online.'

Amazon's Vision is driven by founder Jeff Bezos, who has a well publicised obsession about customer service. He knows that by making it easy for us, we buy more. And this has created the pre-eminent retail business on the planet.

2. It should be simple and memorable

A Vision doesn't have to be long. In fact the shorter and sharper it is, the easier it is to understand and remember.

'To make people happy'

The Disney vision is only four words long, but it sums up perfectly what they are all about.

Their entire focus is on making people happy by watching their movies, visiting their theme parks and buying their merchandise.

And by making people happy, Disney also makes a huge amount of money, which obviously makes their shareholders and employees very happy indeed!

3. It must be realistic and achievable

It's obviously good to have ambition. But if you're a young business and you dream of conquering the world, you really must have something special. Maybe you've invented something, or created an entirely new experience.

That's great, because your ambition must be more than a pipe dream. It must be realistic, and you must have a chance of making it happen.

There are many examples of businesses that have gone from start-up to global leader in a very short time.

Twitter, Facebook, Linkedin, Google and Instagram are all still relatively young businesses, so it's not impossible. It's just that you may need something other than hard work and determination.

If you follow these steps, you will develop an Inspiring Vision that clearly and crisply describes your purpose and ambition.

Here's a very simple structure you can use. You'll need to fill in the blanks with your unique Inspiring Vision.

> "To (define the benefits you deliver to your audience) by (doing whatever your primary purpose and ambition is)."

POWER SUMMARY

Sometimes few words are needed to make a truly big impact!

When first man on the moon Neil Armstrong said *'That's one small step for man, one giant leap for mankind'* it summed up this historic achievement perfectly.

If he'd said, *'Well, here we are'* or *'Wow, we made it!'* I doubt if it would have had the same impact!

So the words you use in any situation must tell a story and have impact.

Back on planet Earth, you need a story that describes what you do. And as I've said before, it must be a clear, concise and compelling story that grabs attention, arouses interest and gets the conversation started.

That's your whole purpose of a Power Summary.

It builds on your Inspiring Vision, and it's ideally less than 50 words.

Now I can hear you ask *'why 50 words?'*

That's an excellent question and the reason is that it should take you no more than 30 seconds to tell your story.

Research shows that the sub-50 word / sub-30 second combination works really well. That's because most humans have a shorter attention span than a Goldfish!

This isn't an insult, it's based on research published in January 2014 by the U.S. National Centre for Biotechnology Information.

It defined attention span as the amount of concentrated time spent on a task without becoming distracted. The key findings were;

- In 2000, average attention span was measured as 21 seconds; in 2013 it was 8 seconds;

- The average attention span of a goldfish is 9 seconds;

- The average person checks their email once every 2 minutes;

The study didn't cover social media but I'll bet if it did, it would show that more and more of us are almost permanently connected to channels like Facebook and Twitter.

The Power Summary is really important because it either starts or kills the conversation. Like the Inspiring Vision, the Power Summary must focus on your audience's interests.

This is the foolproof formula for putting it together;

1. Need

The opportunity you address or problem you solve;

2. Impact

What it means to your audience;

3. Solution

How you address the problem or opportunity;

4. Benefits

What it does for them.

Remember what I said earlier? People are not usually interested in how something works, they are more interested in what it does for them.

Your Power Summary must feel natural, and above all it must be honest and provable. The kiss of death would be for you to get the conversation going and then lose credibility. So resist the temptation to create something sensational just to grab attention, unless of course you can back it up.

Here's something I've made up to illustrate the idea;

'I help small business owners solve the problem of poor cash flow. We all know how damaging late payment is, and my unique service ensures you're paid on time every time.'

If someone you'd never met before said this, what would you say?

Let's look at it a bit closer.

Firstly, it's short and at 31 words speaking in an even tone, you can get through it in around 10 seconds, which is great!

Next it defines the audience as being a small business owner, which may be you.

Then it talks about the problem of late payment and the impact on cash flow. And anyone who runs a business knows how important cash flow is.

If I then say that my service is unique, you could either think *'yeah, right'* or *'what makes it unique?'* In that case you'll want to know why it's unique, how it works and probably what it costs.

You may be the kind of person who has either heard something similar before, or you jump to a conclusion and think 'Debt collector!'

That could be true, but debt collection is hardly unique is it? Maybe it's something else?

If you run a small business and you care about cash flow (and who doesn't!) the chances are high that you'd want to know more.

If you're not interested, it'll probably be because of one or all of the following;

    1. You're not a small business owner;

    2. You don't have that problem;

    3. It seems too good to be true so you don't believe it;

You can do very little about 1 and 2, because not everyone you meet will be your target audience, or have a problem that you address.

You can do something about 3 by working harder on your message.

So let's assume that you've developed a clear, concise and compelling Power Summary. It's hit the mark and sparked interest. The other person then says *'That's interesting, tell me more'* or *'What does that mean exactly?'* Now you've earned the right to start a conversation.

And as we all know, a conversation is not a monologue, it's a two-way exchange of ideas, comments, news and views. This is an ideal opportunity to ask questions (which is always a good idea!) and share information.

It's not an opportunity to unload a pre-prepared sales pitch. Some of that may come later, but first you want to know more about why they are interested. Then you need to develop a relationship based on mutual trust and respect.

And a great way to get this started is to expand your Power Summary to tell them your Engaging Story.

ENGAGING STORY

We all love stories because that's the way we learn.

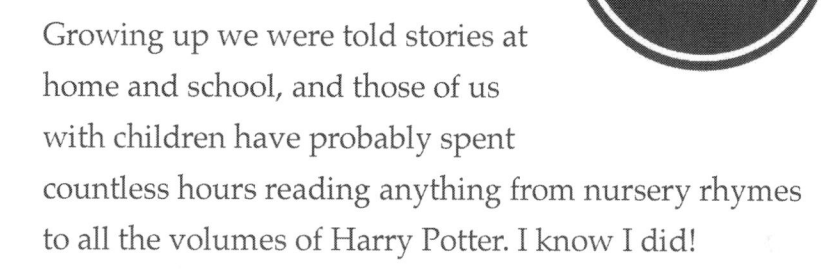

Growing up we were told stories at home and school, and those of us with children have probably spent countless hours reading anything from nursery rhymes to all the volumes of Harry Potter. I know I did!

The Engaging Story expands on the Power Summary and provides more detail. The good thing is that the basic process of creating it is exactly the same. But in this case it's ideally no more than 300-400 words, or one side of an A4 page.

The reason again is down to attention span. Just because you've aroused some interest, it doesn't give you the right to dive in to a long boring monologue.

Your approach should always be to give information in crisp, easily digestible chunks. After all, you don't want to overwhelm the other person and kill the conversation before it gets started, do you?

Of course you don't, you want to build rapport and trust.

They will be sizing you up and deciding how relevant you are to them, and you should be doing exactly the same. Notice that I didn't say 'you need to sell to them!' That's usually the objective, but you must first confirm they have a need you can satisfy. I'll talk about how you can sell to them later.

This is the foolproof formula I've developed for putting an Engaging Story together;

1. Need

2. Impact

3. Solution

4. Benefits

1. Need

You can build on the need and describe it in more graphic terms. This shows that you have a very clear understanding of the issues. It also emphasises why it's really important, and what will happen if it's not addressed.

2. Impact

Here you describe how the problem or opportunity is currently being addressed and what the shortcomings are. You can again explain in graphic terms why these are deficient and why this is a very big problem.

Steve Jobs was a master at this.

In all his major presentations and product launches he identified the problem very well. He always picked a villai, and Apple obviously was the hero who saved the day.

In Apple's 1984 launch of Macintosh, IBM was cast as 'Big Brother' from George Orwell's famous book. The story went like this;

Big Brother (IBM) rules the world, and it controls the way people use computers. In fact it controls their whole existence and experience, and it's dull, boring, grey and soulless. People become automatons who exist on a diet of information Big Brother feeds them.

Surely there must be a better way?

3. Solution

After you've set up the problem (villain) or opportunity, you can now reveal a better way; your unique way of saving the day!

Now you can describe what you do and explain why it's better than the alternatives. You will again want to use graphic language to really emphasise the difference.

Back to Apple's 1984 ad again.

Enter the hero, a young blond lady who tosses a sledgehammer at the screen where Big Brother is speaking to an assembly of followers. His image is shattered and out of the carnage comes Macintosh! Apple saves the world from Big Brother and we all start to 'think differently'. Hooray!

The rest, as they say, is history. Or is it? Maybe in 2014 Apple has become the new Big Brother?

4. Benefits

Now you can describe what's so special about your offer, and why your audience should care. This is where you talk about the unique benefits and value only you can deliver.

In the case of Macintosh, it was a brand new product. Its main attraction was a different user experience. It was a new way of using personal computers and something that many millions of people found irresistible.

The commercial was directed by Ridley Scott of Alien, Gladiator and Blade Runner movie fame. And although it was only ever screened once, at half time during the 1984 Superbowl, it's been hailed as one of the most iconic and best ads ever produced. It also led to more than $150 million in sales of the Macintosh in the first 100 days of its debut. That's small change compared with the way iPads and other devices sell today, but at the time it was hailed as a towering achievement.

If you haven't seen it, it's worth a look. You can find it easily enough by searching online.

Creating a Power Summary and Engaging Story

The Engaging Story is an expanded Power Summary that contains more information to develop the conversation and build trust.

You can use the same structure shown here to develop both.

'I help (audience) to (address problem / opportunity) because (impact statement)

My approach is to (solution statement) which helps you to (benefit statement).'

Now you should have three stunning pieces that you can use in most situations. This is called 'content' and it describes any information that you communicate to the outside world.

What you must now do, is to make sure that you have consistency between everything you publish and use. I call this your Content Library, and that's what I'll cover next.

CONTENT LIBRARY

Your Content Library includes everything about your business, product and service that you publish in the public domain.

This includes brochures, presentations, case studies, sales proposals, social media profiles and website content.

Although you are now developing more detailed work, you should still use the principles I talked about earlier. This is very important, because you want to build on the great start you've made in getting people interested in what you have to say.

One area in which many smaller businesses tend to struggle is design.

This is really important because if you've spent the time creating great content, it must look good.

This isn't about aesthetics though, it's about getting your message across in the best way. This means you make it very easy for people to quickly understand the value of what you do.

But this is where many businesses let themselves down, because they produce pieces in-house and unfortunately they don't look great.

Now I'm not a professional designer, but I've learned a few things about what works and what doesn't.

FONTS

First let's talk about fonts or typefaces.

Most people don't consider these at all, but there's a whole world of design that's devoted to it called Typography.

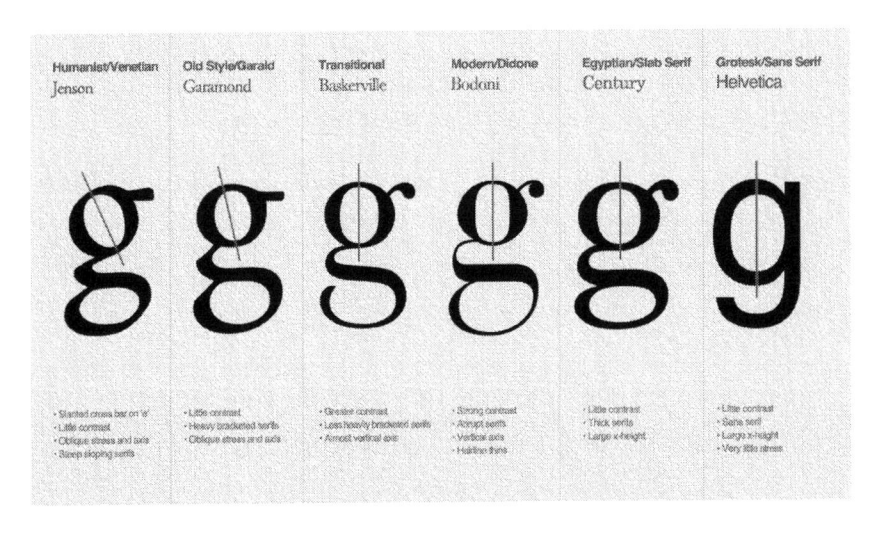

Fonts come in 2 basic types, serif and sans-serif.

Serif fonts have extensions or little stems on the letter, sans-serif don't.

There are literally hundreds of thousands of fonts to choose from, but you can easily find the best ones by doing a simple Google search.

Fonts come in families and within each there are options you can choose from such as light, italic, light italic, bold, regular, extra bold and so on.

The key thing to think about with whatever font you use is readability. In other words, you want your content to be easy to read for anyone. If you pick a family that has many different options, you can use these to make your content really stand out.

You'll notice that in some fonts there are very subtle differences, so it all depends on personal preference.

You can also combine these fonts. For example, you could use a Sans-serif font as a heading and Serif for the body text, or vice-versa. That's what I've done in this book.

My headings all use a Sans-serif font (Lato) and the body text uses a Serif font (Palatino).

I picked them because I think they make it really easy to read what I've written. I also like the look of them and I hope you do too!

The thing is, there is no absolute right or wrong way to do this. But remember, the fonts you use determine how your work looks. That's why you should select a font that portrays the right image for your business.

If I'd used something like the fonts below, I'm sure you agree, it doesn't look as professional or readable as it is now.

MESSAGE STACK

Now I've covered the basics, I want to introduce you to a structure that makes it so much easier to develop messages that will attract attention, and build an audience you can sell to.

COLOURS

Your choice of colours is also important, because this is another major factor in readability.

That's why you should stay away from garish colours that clash. Red lettering on a blue or black background is a very bad idea!

Some colour combinations work very well, and the best are white on black or black on white. This is because there is maximum contrast between them.

The less contrast there is, the harder it becomes to read. You can experiment to see what works best, but take a tip from the magazines and other printed publications you see. Look around you and copy a style that you think works well.

Reinventing the Sale

IMAGES

We all know that a powerful image can make a far bigger, and have a more lasting impact than words alone.

And the more relevant and concrete the image is, the more powerful the effect. That's why an image should not just be decorative. It works best as a visual metaphor which makes or reinforces a point.

When you use images, avoid the free clip art cartoons you can get online. These look awful and they just scream 'cheap!'

This definitely doesn't convey the right image, so always use high quality images if you want to convey a crisp, professional look.

You can get some very good images for free, but be selective. When you search, always use the search tools option in Google to pick the highest quality image. You can also search by colour, type and usage rights. This will show you the images that are free and those you must buy.

There are many sources of reasonably priced stock images such as Fotolia, iStockphoto and Shutterstock.

However, if you don't want to use stock images and you have a good camera, why not create your own?

This can be a great option, because you'll then have something that's totally unique and personal.

WORKSHEET

These questions have been designed in a sequence that gives you the basic raw material you need to create your own Message Stack.

Answer them honestly and use the output as a starting point. Then edit ruthlessly and apply the principles I covered earlier to make your messages as clear, concise and compelling as possible.

If you get stuck on any point, go back and revisit the section that relates to the question.

- **Why does your business exist?**

    What's your 'big idea'?

    What problem does it solve?

    What opportunity does it enable?

- **Why is it different?**

    What are the benefits?

- **Who cares about it?**

    Why do they care?

    Why are they motivated to solve it?

    Why would they do business with you?

- **What do you care about most?**

    How does this affect your audience, partners and employees?

    What impact does your business have on the world?

    What impact do you want it to have?

    What do you most want to be know for?

- **What does success mean to you?**

    How do you measure it?

- **What are your ambitions?**

    Where do you see the business in 12 months and 3 years from now?

    What do you need to do to get there?

SECTION TWO
Strategy

HOW TO BUILD AN AUDIENCE TO SELL TO

Every business needs a plan to focus attention on achieving goals. And the easier this is to understand, the more chance you'll have to execute it.

You have a great idea and you've created messages that really make it stand out. That's great, but now you must take the covers off and tell the world!

And the best way of doing that, is to create a simple strategy that delivers results fast.

This section covers two areas ;

1. Creating a marketing strategy - sometimes called go to market plan;

2. Building an audience - sometimes called lead generation or pipeline development.

This may sound easy but it's an area that so many people get wrong. They either over complicate it or they have no strategy at all. They just 'go with the flow!'

That may sound like a romantic notion, but it's the recipe for disaster. But before I get into how you create a strategy, I'm going to talk about why you need one.

WHY YOU NEED A STRATEGY

There are two simple reasons why developing a plan is a stunningly good idea;

> 1. It provides focus so you spend more time on goal-related activities.
> *The more you focus on a goal, the better your chance of achieving it.*
>
> 2. It removes guesswork and introduces more certainty into your business.
> *When you have goals to measure performance against, you can clearly see how well you're doing.*

I'm sure you know that you need a strategy. But perhaps you're not clear about the best way to create one.

That's why I want to get you to move from planning your work to working you plan as fast as possible, because that's what drives success.

So let's get started!

ASSESSING OPORTUNITY

To run a successful business you need a viable market with good potential. Stagnant, saturated or declining markets are not good unless you can reinvigorate or revolutionise them with a new product or service.

So the first thing you want to do is to confirm (or re-confirm) that you have a great opportunity. And the best way to do this is through an opportunity assessment.

This is a high level exercise, so don't worry too much about detailed analyses and market forecasts at this stage. You may even need to make assumptions, especially if you're bringing something new to market and there's little hard data to look at.

The assessment asks six questions to help you make a decision.

1. What problem are you solving?

You could either be satisfying demand or creating it. This means you either solve a problem or you are introducing something that people will want, need and ultimately buy. Summarise this in the crispest way possible, ideally in a few sentences. Think about it as a Power Summary.

2. Who else provides a solution?

The aim here is to understand who your potential competitors are. This is important because unless you can develop a competitive advantage, you'll find it hard to win business.

- Who are the major competitors?

- How can you gain competitive advantage?

- Why would people do business with you?

3. Why is there an opportunity for you?

Many businesses fail because they just float an idea they hope will succeed. They spend time, effort and money on launching something and then hoping for the best. Unless you get lucky you'll fail, so you must clearly understand why there's an opportunity for you.

- Is there a gap in the market you can exploit?

- What can you deliver that's different?

4. How much revenue can it generate?

This is a very important piece because an idea that doesn't generate revenue isn't much of a business. It's more a hobby!

Of course there's no foolproof way to be certain about this, but it's a good idea to identify the number of potential buyers you could sell to. Then multiple this by the average sales value minus the cost of sale. This formula is simple and it can give you a very good idea of potential revenues;

No. of buyers x average sales value + ongoing revenues + other income - cost of sale

5. What's the time to revenue?

Some businesses have a great idea, but they fail because they run out of money. Cash flow (or the lack of it) kills them.

That's why you must understand how long it will take your idea to generate cash and make a profit!

List the things you must do to get your idea to market. Include all development, marketing, sales and logistics costs, and compare this with potential revenue to arrive at a high level view of profit.

6. Is this a good idea?

Most business people are by nature optimistic. This is good because there will be trying times when you need to look on the bright side.

However, in this case you must assess the opportunity in measurable terms and don't just go on gut instinct. This does sometimes work, but the risk of failure can be high.

If you do go on instinct, at least try to back it up with some facts and never take a totally blind risk, especially if your entire business depends on it.

If it all looks good and you feel positive about the idea, it's time to create a plan.

CREATING THE PLAN

My approach in everything is to keep it as simple as possible. That's why I've produced a format to help you create a go to market strategy. It's called Blueprint and it has 6 parts;

1. Business Model

The different ways you generate revenue;

2. Goals

What you want to achieve;

3. Audience

Who you want to sell to;

4. Channels

The different ways you can sell your product or service;

5. Forces

Things that can affect your performance;

6. Actions

What you must do to succeed.

Reinventing the Sale

BLUEPRINT STRATEGY MODEL

BUSINESS MODEL

In simple terms a business model is the way you generate revenue.

The price someone is prepared to pay for something, reflects what it's worth to them. That's why setting the price can be tricky.

There are many ways you can generate revenue but not all of them will fit every business. In fact you may often have different business models for different groups.

At the most fundamental level any business model is either about volume or price.

If you sell a relatively low value item, you will need to sell it in large volumes. On the flip side, high priced items usually sell at lower volumes. But that's not always the case!

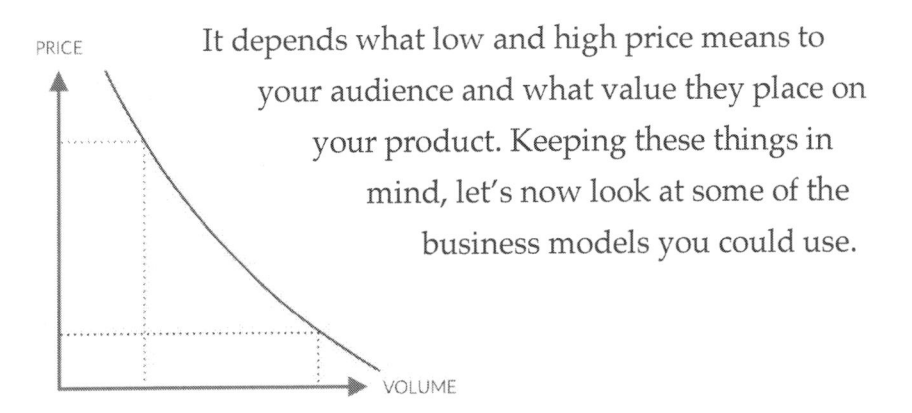

It depends what low and high price means to your audience and what value they place on your product. Keeping these things in mind, let's now look at some of the business models you could use.

Cost plus

This is the most basic model, where you add a margin to what it costs you to make the product or service ready for sale.

A cost plus pricing strategy is easy to put into practice. You know all your costs are covered, so you should be profitable.

However, your margin could be squeezed if your competitors drop their prices and you follow them. Obviously you don't want to sell at a loss, but there may be situations where you do this and recoup your margin later on. This is called a 'Lock-in' strategy.

Lock-in

This is where a very low price, or free offer is designed to lock the buyer into future purchases.

A good example is the mobile phone model, where you get a 'free' handset (worth several hundred pounds) if you sign up for a 2 year subscription plan.

Operators initially lose money by giving the handset away, but they recoup this (and more) over the life of the agreement.

The model was initially developed in 1904, by a gentleman called King C Gillette, who sold the first disposable razor blades.

He decided to give away (or sell at a very steep discount) the actual razor itself. The user obviously needed blades to put in the razor and these were sold separately. This effectively 'locked' the user into the Gillette system and as along as they use the shaver, they had to buy the blades from Mr Gillette.

This approach is now widely used for many other products and services. The price of a good quality inkjet printer has dropped to insanely low levels, but the price of ink is still very high.

In fact, a recent survey by Which magazine showed that on average, ink is more than three times the cost, per millilitre of Dom Perignon Champagne.

The ink costs 51 pence per millilitre, while the champaign costs around 15 pence per millilitre!

Free

This is common with digital products such as software or media. The basic idea is to provide access to a product or service either for a limited time, or with a cut-down set of features. The aim is to let people try before they buy. They can then judge what it's worth to them, before they part with any cash.

Some people will always stay as free users, but others will pay. If you get this balance right, the paying users will effectively subsidise the free users and you still make money.

This is obviously easier to do with digital products, because once you've produced your app, ebook or training programme, the ongoing costs are very small. It's probably only the annual hosting fees to maintain a website plus time and other overheads. This is different to a physical product, which will have a unit cost of production and distribution.

Some businesses support their free strategy through advertising, sponsorship and affiliate marketing (selling someone else's product), but you must be careful with this because it could easily detract from your original purpose.

Value Added

This is where your prices vary with the value delivered; the greater the value, the higher the price. This is used mainly when selling services.

A good example of this is a client I recently worked with. They provide a consultancy service that helps organisations to reduce cost. They charge a small initial fee to set it up, then they take a percentage of the savings achieved.

This is sometimes called 'Risk-Reward' or 'Gain-share' and it can be very profitable. However, you must agree on the baseline you start from and the steps that trigger payment.

Competitive

This is where you deliberately set your prices against the competition, or they set theirs against you.

You could be aggressive and offer the same or better capabilities at a lower price. Be careful though because if you start a price war with a bigger competitor, they could drop prices to levels that you can't match. And that's a rapid way to go out of business.

But be careful about competing purely on the basis of cost. It's a better idea to show the added-value you deliver. If you do some important things that they don't, you should be able to charge a premium. That's assuming these things are important and of value to the buyer.

Combination strategies

In practice many businesses combine elements of several different strategies.

Whatever you decide to do though, the key thing is to make sure you are profitable. Remember the old saying;

> "Revenue is vanity, profit is sanity."

Things change, so you should be agile and adapt when it makes business sense. So just a quick summary on business models to reinforce the key points;

- Price and value are inextricably linked;

- You may have many business models;

- Use the best model for each group;

- Make it easy for people to buy;

- Be creative but always profitable.

GOALS

Goals are the key drivers of your strategy and the benchmarks against which progress is measured.

Some organisations set long-range goals for years into the future. Although none of us can see the future, some believe they can create it. And there are good examples of companies who have done this by introducing new products and services that created demand. When Apple introduced iPad it created a category called tablets, which it quickly dominated. So if you have a killer idea that will do something similar, factor it into your plan.

It's good to dream big as long as you are not deluding yourself. However you must have a hard focus on what you can achieve this year. That's why I suggest you create a plan that covers the next 12 months. In reality, this is all most of us can handle any way.

Be specific and set actual targets. For example rather than say 'increase sales', say 'increase sales by 15% by December 31st'.

This is important because a goal of 'being the best in the UK' can't accurately be measured. This is really more of a wish than a true goal.

You must also make sure your goals are realistic and achievable. A good way to check this is to ask a few key questions;

- Can you achieve them with the resources you currently have?

- Do you need more people, cash or equipment?

- Do you have people with the right skills?

- Can you fund growth yourself or do you need investment?

These things must be factored into your thinking because they could be constraints on achieving your goals.

You can have as many goals as you like, but fewer may be better. It's also useful to break goals down into time periods, so that you can monitor progress. Whether this is annually, quarterly, monthly or weekly is up to you.

AUDIENCE

You must also be clear about who you are selling to. This is important because you want to create messages that will attract their attention.

- Are you selling to business, the professions, public sector, government, the general public or specific niches?

- Who are the people you sell to? What are their roles and responsibilities?

- What are their pressing needs, concerns and ambitions?

- What are they interested in?

- Are there new markets or sectors you could sell into?

Even if you sell a mass-market product, you can still break your audience into different groups and target them with specific messages.

Mobile phone companies do it, which is why you see models specifically designed to appeal to different age groups.

Car makers also do it with vehicles like the Smart that's aimed at urban dwellers, because it's perfectly designed for zooming around a city and parking in tight spaces. When you've defined your target audience, you will want to define the best channels to use to reach them.

CHANNELS

There are three main models for taking your product to market;

- Online
- Direct
- Indirect

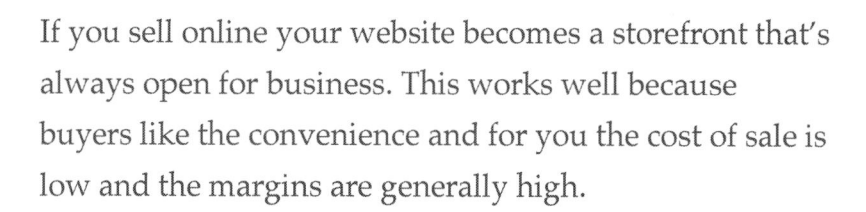

If you sell online your website becomes a storefront that's always open for business. This works well because buyers like the convenience and for you the cost of sale is low and the margins are generally high.

If you sell direct you will have salespeople meeting potential buyers. This can be expensive and sales cycles are often longer.

If you work indirectly through partners or agents, your cost of sale may be lower, but you also have less control over their performance.

Partners are seen as an extension of your business, so you must make sure they have the qualities you are looking for. The obvious things include;

- A vested interest in, and a commitment to selling your product or service;

- A good understanding of the markets you sell into;

- Great people who will represent you in the right way;

- Proven track record of sales expertise;

- An excellent reputation for delivering great service;

- A willingness to work with you on joint initiatives to win business and support customers;

- Providing feedback and input to help you improve your products and services.

The best relationships are based on mutual gain. That's why partners must be motivated to work with you. Clearly, if they can build a successful business by working with you, they will be highly motivated, which is exactly what you want from a partner.

The aim is to find the right balance between different routes to market, that creates a great customer experience and maximises your revenue.

Many organisations of course adopt a multi-channel strategy. But this needs a bit of thought, because you will want to avoid any channel conflict.

An example of channel conflict is where you are selling to someone both directly and through a partner, and it's not clear what the best for the client is.

Obviously you don't want to compete against partners who are selling your products. And you certainly don't want to sell through different channels at different prices.

To prevent this you must define the basis on which partners sell your products. This should include the financial details of your relationship (the margins for selling your product) and how you expect them to represent you.

Some products are obviously best sold face to face, whilst others are perfect online.

When considering what approach works best for you, the key questions should always be;

- How can I provide a great customer experience?
- How can I make it easy for people to buy?
- Does this make financial sense?

Making it easy for people to buy is important as long as you make a profit!

The fact is, the easier you make it for people to buy, the more they will generally buy.

The next thing to consider are the things that can either help you succeed, or cause you problems and I call these Forces.

FORCES

In business there are good (or positive) forces that can help you to succeed, and bad (or negative) forces that can cause you to fail

So you either need to harness the force and use it to your advantage, or neutralise it.

There are some forces that you can directly control such as;

- Strategy;
- Products and services;
- People;
- Culture and organisation.

There are others that you can't such as:

- Competitors;
- The economy;
- Legislation;
- Political and social events;
- Natural disasters.

Although you may be able to influence some of them, your focus should be on what you can directly control. And you also need to be able to react to the others.

To help create the right focus, I've split forces into 2 groups - internal and external.

Internal forces

These are normally the things you can directly control. So you must understand which forces are good and which are bad. Then you will want to improve the bad, and make the good even better.

You obviously will want to build and sustain strong sales growth, and the best way to do this is to implement the right strategy. I think about this like building a house.

```
          INSPIRATIONAL
      MANAGEMENT & LEADERSHIP
    ┌─────────────────┬─────────────────┐
    │    EXCELLENT    │      GREAT      │
    │     PEOPLE      │    PRODUCTS     │
    ├─────────────────┼─────────────────┤
    │    THE RIGHT    │     STRONG      │
    │    STRUCTURE    │     CULTURE     │
    ├─────────────────┴─────────────────┤
    │        SALES-LED STRATEGY         │
    └───────────────────────────────────┘
```

All successful businesses are sales-led, which means they focus on their audience and provide a great buying experience.

So the first building block is to develop a sales-led strategy and by following this programme, that's exactly what you'll be doing.

The next thing you need is an organisational structure that supports that strategy. This means having the right people in the right roles.

It also means creating a structure that helps you to share ideas and make rapid, informed decisions. Agility is important because things change fast and the successful businesses adapt quickly.

Culture is also critically important because you want to get the very best from your people. In my experience, even in large businesses, an open culture that encourages people to actively express their thoughts and ideas always works best.

It's a fact that when people feel happy they generally do great work. You can create this by building a strong team ethic people that encourages people to work for, rather than against each other. If you develop the right environment to delight your customers and grow your team, your chances of success are dramatically improved.

Great products are key to your success because that's what people buy. But you need people with the right skills to sell them. This means hiring the talent you need, and also developing the talent you have.

These are really key assets that you must continue to develop to build and sustain that strong sales growth.

Lastly is the fact that you must have leaders who can bring this all together to drive the strategy and direction of the business and deliver results.

There are many examples of great leaders in all walks of life who made a difference. These leaders all succeeded because they united people behind a common cause.

You may not be the next Alex Ferguson, Steve Jobs or Jack Welch, but you can learn from them. There is certainly no shortage of reading material available!

External forces

Let's now talk about those forces that are often outside your control. These include many different things that can have an impact on your business. Some of these can be very positive and profitable and others negative and damaging.

Your task is to understand these forces and develop the right strategy to address them. You will want to understand what impact a particular market force is likely to have on buying behaviour, and whether this is something you can take advantage of.

Let's consider a market force called the Y2K or Millennium 'bug'. This was a combined technology and market driven force that spread fear of doom, with the imminent collapse of computer systems all over the globe.

The problem was caused because most hardware and software was designed in a way that meant it would stop working as the year 2000 dawned. It was considered a significant and real threat to our very survival.

There was widespread fear that aircraft would fall from the sky, and traffic would grind to a halt across the planet as computers stopped working.

Far from being doom and gloom, for many IT businesses it was 'boom and boom' as they developed a wide range of 'Y2K services' that anxious organisations all over the world bought. Recent estimates place the expenditure on this at over it $300 billion!

Let's also consider the ever-present threat of competition.

Your job is to understand what your competitors do, and then help your audience clearly understand what makes you different.

Assessing where you are in the competitive landscape is obviously an important factor in deciding your strategy. The problem is that most markets are intensely competitive, so it's easy to get bogged down with analysis. It's also difficult to make an objective assessment of how you are really positioned against competitors.

The key factor you should consider is not absolute size but momentum, because this determines who is consistently winning business.

Competitors with momentum are the most dangerous.

Some companies drive momentum through product and service innovation, whilst others achieve it through a focus on performance.

Here's a way to look at this that I call the Competitive Momentum grid. It evaluates your relative position based on four kinds of momentum.

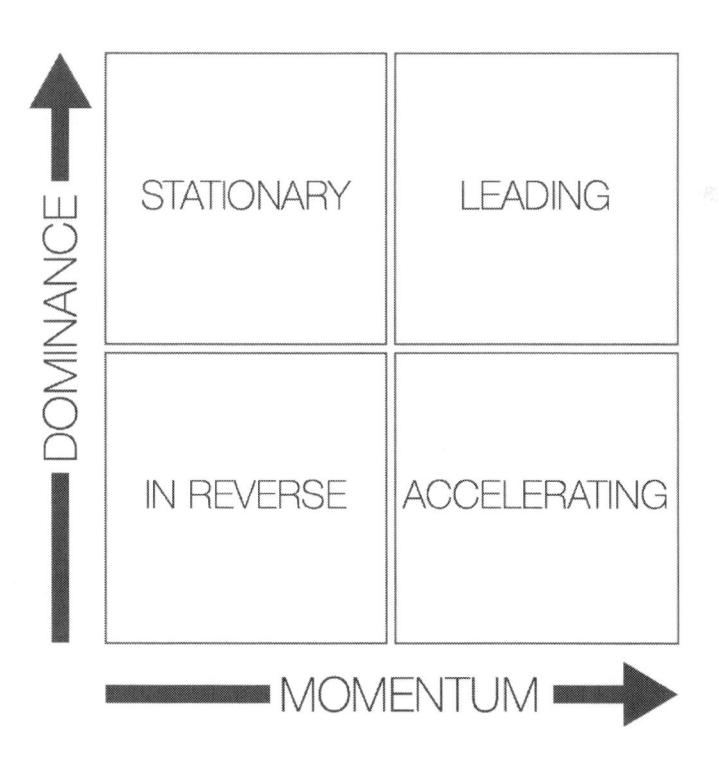

	STATIONARY	LEADING
DOMINANCE ↑		
	IN REVERSE	ACCELERATING

MOMENTUM →

In reverse

Means you are going backwards due to one or more factors such as poor performance, an uncompetitive product, lack of innovation and failure to adapt to change.

Stationary

Means you are standing still.

Accelerating

Means you are winning more and more business, and making up ground fast through innovation or execution.

Leading

Means you consistently win the business you bid for and you see strong and sustained growth. You are regarded as one of the top businesses in your sector and a preferred supplier to many customers.

When you've added the key competitors, position yourself.

If you are in reverse or stationary, how are you going to improve your position?

This is a big question but the answer could be simple. You may be in trouble because your service isn't as good as it should be. Or perhaps you are missing opportunities because you're not aware of them, or competing in enough sales opportunities.

These are relatively easy to fix and this book series will help you to pinpoint the issues. You must then commit to taking the right action to correct them to get back on track.

If you are accelerating or leading, congratulations!

Your business is doing well. Now you need to think about how you maintain your position. Things can change fast and you must be able to respond to threats to your position.

Driving growth is one thing, sustaining it is what builds a successful long-term business.

This section has covered a lot of ground, so let's briefly summaries the key points

On Forces

- Forces can help or hurt you;
- Some you control, others you manage;
- Internal forces are directly in your control;
- Set the right strategy to drive growth;
- Create the conditions to achieve success;
- Rapidly adapt to opportunity and risk.

On strategy

- Develop a strategy to focus on priorities;
- Have or create an opportunity to pursue;
- Set simple, realistic and achievable goals;
- Define your target audience;
- Create the right business models and channels;
- Make it easy for people to buy;
- Continually improve to drive and sustain growth.

WORKSHEET

Goals

- What do you want to achieve this year?

- What can stop you?

- How can you overcome this?

- Can you achieve your goals with current resources?

- Where are the gaps?

- How will you fill them?

Business model

- What's your current business model?

- What are your sources of revenue?

- How can they be improved?

- Have you looked at competitors models?

- Have you looked at models from other sectors?

- What can you learn from them?

Audience

- Are there new or emerging sectors to sell into?
- How well do you understand their needs?
- Why are you a good fit?
- Do you have a plan to address them?
- What's the potential revenue?
- Is your idea ready to go or does it need work?
- How long will it take?
- What costs are involved?

Channels

- How do you sell today?
- What works best?
- What's the most profitable?
- What's the ideal profile of a partner?
- How well do partners perform?
- Why would partners work with you?
- What's your partner value proposition?

- Do you have joint goals?
- Do you have joint plans?
- How important are you to each other's success?
- What happens if the relationship ceases today?
- What is the overall value of the relationship to you and them?

Forces

- Is your business sales-led?
- Is there clear responsibility for key areas such as sales, operations, development and support?
- Is there strong leadership and a clear vision?
- Is there a leader who provides motivation and inspiration?
- Is the culture open and flat or closed and hierarchical?
- How well does the organisation work as a team?
- Does it support effective decision making?
- Are the right people in the right roles?

Market forces

- What are the key business trends?

- What are the drivers of buying behaviour?

- What are the factors that motivate people to buy?

- What changes are happening in sectors you sell into?

- What impact does this have for your business?

- Is it something that can help or hinder your efforts?

- How is it likely to affect buying behaviour?

- Can you harness this to drive demand for your product or service?

- What do you need to do to capitalise on the opportunity?

Competitive landscape

- Where do you fit in the competitive landscape?
- Who do you admire most and why?
- Who do you fear most and why?
- Who would you like to emulate and why?
- What's your competitive advantage?
- What makes you unique?
- What can you deliver that others can't?
- Who can you collaborate with?

EXECUTING THE PLAN

So you've created a go to market plan that you're happy with. You're clear about what you want to achieve, and you're confident you're in good shape to do it. Now it's time to take action and build an audience you can sell to.

This is often called pipeline development or lead generation. And for many businesses this is where the problems start. They use so called tried and tested techniques such as email or cold-calling to pitch their ideas to people they hope will buy from them.

The problem is that most of these techniques are outdated. They don't work well in today's connected world, where buyers are more informed than ever.

So rather than pitch at people, you must connect with them and share information they'll be interested in.

People buy to solve a problem.

They don't buy something for what it is, they buy it for what it does for them. So before you can sell a solution, you must build trust with your audience.

That's really important, because they want to feel confident that you know what you're talking about. And when they do trust you enough, they'll be more likely to do business with you.

We live in an age of global mass communication and several billion people have access the internet. That means that we can now reach more people on the planet than ever before.

That's quite an amazing thought!

Obviously not all of them will be your audience so you must be selective.

In this section I'm going to talk about the different ways you can start a conversation with your audience.

I'll focus on the key channels of communication that you can use.

Although not all of them may be right for you, it's a good idea to experiment to see what works best.

1. WEBSITE

Every business needs some kind of online presence, because most of us get our information online.

In fact, one of the first things we all do is to Google someone we don't know. So even if you don't actually sell online, you must have a credible online profile. If you don't, people will be reluctant to trust you. And that makes establishing a relationship very difficult.

But being online doesn't necessarily mean having your own website. You can build a credible online presence with sites like About.Me, Amazon, Blogger, eBay, Facebook, Google+, LinkedIn, Pinterest, Squidoo, Tumblr, Twitter and Youtube.

The drawback is that you have no direct control over the way these sites look. You can customise your page, but the site owner always has ultimate control.

They can make changes and even shut you down without notice. So relying on these as your primary online profile, is probably not a good idea.

But using them to supplement your own website is a great idea. It means you will show up more in searches, which obviously enhances your online reputation.

Having your own site does however bring a level of credibility to your business. It also means that you can create your own unique identity, and you also have total control over how you project yourself.

Whatever you choose though, remember that this is your shop window. People will make judgements on what they see and that's why you must pay special attention to anything you post online. Those embarrassing videos or photos you posted on Facebook may well come back to haunt you!

There are two options for creating your own site.

1. Do it yourself

2. Hire someone

1. Do it yourself

This is actually not as scary or difficult as it sounds. You don't need to know HTML code or Javascript (these are the programming languages you use to create websites) because there are tools that take care of this.

There are many template driven site builders that you can use such as Moonfruit, Yola, Create and Wix.

These enable you to create a site from a range of templates. You just add your own words and images into a defined layout and off you go!

Your site is hosted by the company and you pay a monthly fee to keep your site going. The potential downside is that these tools are pretty simple so you may feel limited by the lack of flexibility in some of them. The costs range from free to several hundred pounds a year.

Free is rarely a good idea though, because you may have adverts on your site or limited space or features. It also generally looks like a cheap (free) site, so if you want to create a good business-like image, be prepared to pay.

If you decide you need more control, or would even like to try your hand at website design and build your own, there are again, many options available.

Here are some of the best; some are free like Drupal and Wordpress (this is called Open-Source software) and others you pay for.

In my view, the 3 best tools you can use are Dreamweaver, Wordpress and Rapidweaver.

Dreamweaver is a very popular tool that non-professionals can learn to use. However it may be a bit expensive and complicated for the complete novice user.

Wordpress is a very popular platform with many free templates you can use to create an individual look. There are also premium themes that are more sophisticated and offer more scope.

Rapidweaver (no relation to Dreamweaver) is a simple but very powerful tool that runs only on the Apple Mac computer platform. It's about a quarter of the cost of Dreamweaver and it's very easy to learn.

Of course the more you know the better you become. But you may not have the time or desire to do this. In that case you pay someone to build a site for you.

2. Hire someone

The big advantage is that you are buying expertise, which means your site will probably look very good, and it will be live faster than if you do it yourself.

The potential downside is that it will be more expensive than doing it yourself. And you will also have to rely on someone else to make changes. The costs can mount up, but for many, this is a price worth paying.

Key attributes

Whether you do it yourself or hire someone, there are certain things your site must have.

1. It must be sticky

Visitors should be encouraged to go deep into your site. You do this by developing content that's clear, concise and compelling because this grabs their attention.

2. It must be simple

The site must be clean with a layout that allows your great content to shine through. Keep things as simple as possible and eliminate anything that doesn't add to the visitor experience.

Always use super clear navigation to make it easy for visitors to find the information they need, and quickly get around the site.

Also make it as easy as possible for visitors to connect with you. Allow them to send you a message from any page and only ask for essential information on contact forms. Don't ask for too much too soon, because people will happily share more information when they trust you.

3. It must look great

The web is a visual medium and your site must stand out, look different and be really easy to use.

So it's best to avoid fancy navigation or other design features that may look cool, but confuse the visitor.

If you have the skills to do it in-house that's great, but if you don't, work with the best designer you can afford. Then challenge them to produce something you absolutely love. You should be proud of your site and keen to show it off!

Remember that this is your shop window and if it looks a mess, you create a really bad impression that turns people off. This obviously makes it hard to build trust, which really does defeat the whole purpose!

2. EMAIL

Every day more than 300 billion email messages are sent

That's more than 3 million every second!

Email is everywhere, and everyone almost without exception uses it as part of their daily life.

Although email is sometimes seen as an old-fashioned alternative to social media, it's still the most widely used method of communication.

And that's why it's a very important tool for building a network. But over the years email marketing has developed an image problem. As soon as you say 'email marketing', many people think 'spam'.

That's because it's been used and abused by people who mass mail anyone, in the hope that they get some interest.

Are you an email spammer?

Here are tell-tale signs that you either are a fully fledged spammer, or verging on it;

- You send bulk email through an email programme;

- You buy or rent a mailing list;

- Your message heavily promotes your product;

- There is no unsubscribe link on your email;

- Your main concern is how many opt-outs and bounces you get, rather than the value you provide;

- You have a contact database segmented into 'blast', 'email' and 'do not email';

- To you, search engine optimisation means more traffic, not better results for visitors;

- You don't know if your contacts are opted in, or what they opted in for;

- You use a fishbowl at conferences to collect business cards and then follow them up with an email.

The reality is that if you spam people by email, you will get nowhere. Actually you may get blacklisted by your internet service provider or mail service, and you'll end up wasting a lot of time, effort and money. Your network will still be empty and you'll get more desperate.

And that's what's called a vicious circle!

DESPAIR

The best way to use email is to send a message to someone who has given you permission to contact them.

But what do you do if you're starting from scratch and you have no contacts? Unless you do something you'll go out of business.

Here's an approach I've used many times that works well;

- Find the right person to contact;
  You can do this through basic research on their website, Google or social media;

- Contact them ideally through a social media channel, via a referral or introduction;
  If that's not possible you will have to make a direct approach;

- Arouse their interest with a message;
  Then ask for permission to send them more information;

- Connect with them;
  And start the conversation.

The message is the most important thing and it must attract attention to help you make progress. The best way to create that message, is to understand what could grab the attention of the person you want to contact.

An internet search can throw up some useful information, and you can also set up a Google Alert.

This will show you where that person is mentioned online, and from this you can build a picture of what they are likely to be interested in.

When you have the key points of interest, you're ready to create and send your email.

Here are the things you must do to maximise the chances of success

- Always address it to a named individual;

- Create an attention grabbing headline that motivates the recipient to open it;

- Make the message personal and relevant to their interest;

- Define what action you want them to take;

- Provide a link to your site, or another place where they can get more information, such as a landing page;

- Tell them how to opt out, and have an unsubscribe link prominently displayed.

If you follow this advice, I guarantee that your emails will be more successful.

A REAL-LIFE EXAMPLE

Whilst working on an interim assignment for a software company, I had an objective to set up a meeting with the Chief Information Officer (CIO) of one of the largest companies in the UK.

I had no connection with him and his company had never done business with my client before. This was a new and totally fresh approach.

He is a prominent, high profile person who frequently speaks at conferences around the world. He is widely regarded as an expert by his peers and he regularly publishes papers. His company has operations all over the world and he travels extensively.

This is obviously a tough nut to crack!

Here's how I secured a meeting with that CIO.

A Google search gave me a lot of information which included;

Press releases, news items and articles where he was mentioned.

Slides he used for presenting at recent conferences and videos of him speaking on his company website.

LinkedIn provided more information on his background.

I looked for points of common ground, and found that he attended the same university that I did.

We also jointly belonged to two LinkedIn groups and I noticed that he'd posted comments a few times.

There was also a link to his personal blog, which gave me even more information.

I started to get a good impression of what he was like and what he was interested in. From this I drew up a list of what I thought his priorities were.

When I'd done this I thought about how we could address them. I wanted to be very clear about why he should care about what we had to say, because this was going to be an important part of my approach.

This is a no-nonsense professional who is intelligent, ambitious and successful. I would have a single shot at making a good impression. If I messed up, there would be no second chance.

To send him an email that he would respond to, I knew I had to ask his permission, so I decided to send him a LinkedIn InMail as a first step.

I wrote a short message and created a headline that I thought would get his attention. It did and he accepted my offer of more information by email.

After a few exchanges and a very brief call, he agreed to a 30 minute meeting at his London office.

Needless to say, I made sure that I was totally prepared for that meeting. It was successful and the start of a relationship that I believe is still going strong today.

This scenario works very well if you are contacting a very small number of people. But what do you do if your target audience is much larger?

That's when social media can be very useful.

3. SOCIAL MEDIA

In the dark and distant days before the internet was everywhere, we connected with one another face-to-face, by letter or by telephone.

Face-to-face was the expectation, but today it's becoming the exception. We now inhabit our own virtual world where we talk to our family and friends. We share news, photos, videos and other aspects of our lives.

Early social websites evolved into social media platforms like Facebook. And then people realised this presented many new ways to make money.

The inevitable abuse and scamming followed until we became smarter at avoiding it.

Then the business world realised that these platforms provided many opportunities for creating influence and power for their brands.

Soon the channels were flooded with advertising as the marketing people moved in. This meant that over time they became just an online version of the things most companies did offline.

'Social Business' and 'Social CRM' then evolved and new software platforms were developed to manage the relationships even more tightly. What was originally open and free, is now rapidly becoming closed and expensive.

Although 'social' is everywhere, many people still don't use it effectively for business. They may have mastered the mechanics of how digital media channels work, but unfortunately they don't have anything significant to say.

There is a theory that if you connect with a large number of people, you will create a vibrant network of valuable business contacts. I don't think that's true, becauseI believe the quality of your network is more important than the quantity.

There's certainly no shortage of social media strategists and guru's who promise instant success in exchange for your attention, email address and ultimately your cash.

There are some wild promises that in many cases turn out to be nothing other than scams. I know these are harsh and cynical words, but consider this;

Social media is not magic ...

It's just another way of connecting to and interacting with people online.

Sites such as Facebook, LinkedIn, Twitter, Google+ and the rest can be a powerful way of building momentum in your business. But only if you use them in the right way.

This doesn't mean understanding how to use the site and post content. It's a lot simpler than that, and I'll get into that in a moment.

But before I do, I want you to understand one thing.

Social media is exactly the same as 'normal' communication. It's just that it enables you to communicate personally with many people simultaneously.

Think about that for just a second.

Personal conversations with many people at the same time. That's real power.

But I see many examples of people abusing that power and getting absolutely nowhere. And I'm talking about large companies as well as small.

It seems as though the normal rules of etiquette and social convention have been ignored. Messages are pushy, self-centred, brash, insincere, poorly written and too good to be true. And many are!

Emails, tweets, blogs and status updates are just boring monologues that push opinions, brands and products at anyone who will listen.

This is a wasted opportunity though, because the real power of social media is in the mass sharing of ideas and content.

But because we live in a world of instant gratification, we want quick fixes for everything. That's why there are so many people who promise you that they can help you build a vast network in a week. They talk about sharing their 'secrets' with you. But what they are doing is selling you a book or a training course.

That's fine if it works, but you have to be very careful and selective.

Of course you can get a network of names by making amazing offers and using dubious marketing tricks. But that's not what I'm talking about if you want to build a quality network. To do that you must create and share meaningful ideas that have real value for others.

Your goal is to draw people towards you through the strength of your ideas and you can do this by following a few simple rules.

Put others first

People are basically self-centred and they care about themselves first. There are exceptions, but this is a generally accepted fact of human nature.

But to truly succeed in business you must reverse this. You must put other's interests ahead of your own. And this is even more important with social media. This is because we are naturally sceptical of people who push their own self interest.

However, many businesses get this wrong because they use social media channels to promote themselves far too early.

We follow famous people because we are interested in what they have to say because we are curious how they live their lives.

But unless you are famous, you will not have the same pulling power. This means you must work hard to build and maintain a following. And you can do this through the strength and originality of your ideas.

So in future, instead of hustling for business, think about how you can genuinely help people. Be interested in others and they will be interested in you.

Smile

The world is a serious place, with conflicts, boom and bust economic cycles and political and social upheaval.

That's why a smile is such a powerful thing. It makes us feel good and we gravitate towards happy, positive people.

It's hard to be negative to someone who is happy, as long as their happiness is sincere.

Insincerity smacks of devious self-interest and it will drive people away very quickly.

When we are face to face with someone, projecting a smile is easy. But in the online world this can difficult, unless you are engaged in real-time with video.

When you communicate through any online medium you must convey the right image. And the way you create a happy feeling in social media, is through the words you use and the way you deliver them.

This is called 'tone of voice' and it's really important because people form an opinion of you based on this. This means using a positive tone with upbeat words, rather than dull, boring and negative words.

But keep this in balance. Don't use unbelievably sensationalist words purely for effect. Remember that you must be able to prove any claims you may make, so always be truthful.

You should always avoid any downbeat comment or negative sentiment in your written words. There are many examples of people who have tweeted inadvisable, knee-jerk comments they have later regretted.

Of course an apology can be issued and comments retracted, but these things can spread like wildfire and it's difficult to repair the damage. Be upbeat and positive and you will attract people to you.

Make it personal

Social media enables you to have personal conversations with many different people at the same time.

That's why you must always send messages and connection requests to people and use their name.

Our name is really important. It's personal to us, and if it's not used correctly it can cause offence and get the intended relationship off to a shaky start.

Never ever send a message through any medium with the dreaded 'dear friend' because there is just no excuse other than laziness.

Don't be too personal either, and never use a nick name or call Victoria, Vicky or Charles, Charlie, unless you've been introduced to them, or they've introduced themselves in that way. If they have an unusual name always check the spelling.

If you're in any doubt, check to see how they refer to themselves on their website, blog or other platform. Or better still, ask someone who knows them what they like to be called.

Being too formal is as bad as being too informal, and once you've set the scene it's difficult to go back.

Making it personal sets the tone of the relationship you'd like to build. Start in the right way and build from there.

As well as getting their name right, alway personalise your invitation. Tell them why you want to connect and how they will benefit if they do.

For example, never use the standard LinkedIn invitation, because this shows you can't be bothered to think about their needs. I know most people still accept the invitation, but that's probably because;

- They can't be bothered to reject it;
- They don't want to be rude;
- It's quick and easy to just hit the accept button.

Remember, it's not the quantity of connections that matters, it's the quality.

Listen more

The ability to listen is a real competitive advantage. This is because people are so busy promoting themselves, they just don't listen to what others are saying.

When you listen you can convert connections into relationships. But only if you are meaningful to them and you provide value.

Use social media to understand and confirm issues, needs and desires and then talk about your unique perspective on them.

This is when you start to build the relationship. By listening it shows that you're interested in what the other person has to say, rather than selfishly pushing your own agenda. You can also ask and answer questions by participating in groups on platforms like LinkedIn.

Make your comments relevant and not just a loaded question that's related to your self-interest. Most people are smart enough to see through that, and the response will be poor.

Use social media to listen and you may be surprised at what you learn.

Sit in their seat

To be relevant you must discuss what matters to your audience and you can't do that unless you put yourself in their place.

The problem is that much of social media marketing is concerned only with adding another follower or adding another LinkedIn connection.

Many people use social media as a monologue, which is like throwing mud against a wall and hoping some of it sticks.

Your goal should be to build a relationship based on trust and you will only do this by demonstrating relevance and value. And remember, your products are only relevant if they solve a problem or a desire.

So rather than trying to develop thousands of 'friends', develop smaller and stronger groups that matter.

Whether you create a message, make an invitation or post an update, ask yourself how you would react if you were the recipient.

Before you make contact, think about what's in it for the other person and ask yourself why they should respond.

Make a difference

Leave people better off from the experience of connecting with you. Try to enrich their lives in some way, or give them something they didn't have before they met you.

Make an impact on their world, and they will remember you and possibly want to reciprocate. Change your attitude and move away from being manipulative to being meaningful.

Think about adding value rather than trying to continually extract it. Be genuinely interested, kind, considerate and compassionate and you will win through. Be totally self-centred, greedy and pushy and people will ignore you.

Of course there are no guarantees that this works every time, because it won't.

Sometimes people will take from you and not reciprocate, but that's life.

However, it is worth sticking to your task and thinking about how you can make a difference, rather than how you can just make money.

If you do the first, the second will usually follow.

Many people use social media to sell hard from the start. That may work in some cases, but you can stand out by not doing those things.

You can draw people towards you by making a difference to their lives.

You can attract enquiries and get referrals because people like you and trust you.

And that's how to get better results with social media.

4. THE TELEPHONE

The phone has been around for more than a century and although it's come a long way, the basic purpose is unchanged.

Before the internet caught on, the phone was the primary means of communication in business and 'Telemarketing' became an accepted technique for generating sales leads.

I remember when I first started in sales.

I was fresh out of university, armed with a degree and I decided that selling would be a breeze!

Then the reality kicked in! It was tough.

Very tough.

I had no leads, just a territory, company car, a copy of yellow pages and a phone.

It was a big wake up call and the only way I had of creating sales leads, was to visit companies and leave a business card, brochure, or make a phone call.

I did both and it was hard, but I did make progress. It was also a very steep learning curve.

That was more than 30 years ago and things have moved on. Or have they?

What amazes me, is that many businesses still adopt the same approach today! This is just plain stupid though because it doesn't work any more.

There are other, far more effective ways of connecting with people. Cold-calling is a nuisance and that's exactly why it rarely works. In fact, unsolicited calls are now banned in many countries.

Most of the cold-calling today is pretty bad because the smarter companies have abandoned it. Unfortunately there are many less-smart ones, who still think sales is a numbers game. They believe that the more calls you make, the more likely you are to succeed. But that's just not true!

How to use the phone in the right way

However the phone still has a valuable role to play when it's used correctly. It's excellent for following up on a request for information, making invitations to events and calling a referral. So everyone should be able to use it in the right way. Here are a few things to bear in mind that will help;

Before you call

- Be very clear about the purpose of your call;

- Think about what's in it for the person you are calling;

- Draft a short agenda for the call;
  Make a few notes on what you want to say, and the questions you want to ask;

  Create an attention grabbing introduction;

- Anticipate likely questions and plan your response;
  Think about how they will respond to your call;

  What are the most probable questions they will have?

  Don't use a script or learn a speech because this will sound insincere;

When you call

- Always be professional and personable;

- Strike the right balance between being friendly and happy, but don't be familiar or too enthusiastic;

- Politely introduce yourself, briefly state the purpose of your call, and ask if now is a convenient time to talk;
  This is just basic good manners. Truly bad calls are where people just plough on with their speech and hardly draw breath! If now is not a good time, arrange to call back;

- Establish rapport quickly;
  Ask questions in a conversational way and let them answer;

  Encourage them to talk, even if it's to tell you to go away!

- Never pressure anyone;
  Don't try to close them on the phone;

  Respect their time and keep your questions and comments short.

- Listen for clues;
  Be aware if it seems that they don't want to talk, or if they seem preoccupied;

If that's the case ask if it would be more convenient to call later and then rearrange the call;

- Always close on an action;
Confirm what you've agreed and follow up with an email;

If there's no interest, ask if they want to be taken off your list or not contacted in future;

Thank them for their time and close.

And that's a very simple guide to help you use the phone in the most effective way.

5. DIRECT MAIL

Direct mail covers anything that you physically send someone. It could be a letter, parcel, samples, DVD or anything that you use to attract attention and try to build a relationship.

Direct Mail is sometimes called 'snail mail' because it takes so long! It certainly takes longer than digital messages, it's far more expensive and it also takes much more effort to produce and get in the hands of your audience.

But research shows that it can be effective, if you use it selectively.

Let me be very clear here though. I'm not advocating you send thousands of leaflets, or junk mail. I'm talking about low volume and personalised mail.

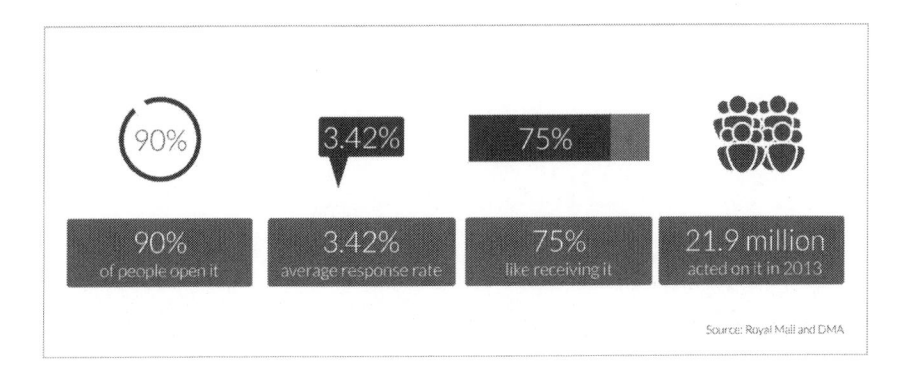

90%	3.42%	75%	21.9 million
of people open it	average response rate	like receiving it	acted on it in 2013

Source: Royal Mail and DMA

You see there's value in rarity.

So when everyone uses email, social media or the phone, you can stand out by doing something different. It shows that you've taken more time and effort.

It's similar to those eCards that are now popular at Christmas. I may be old fashioned, but that shows absolutely no thought. A hand-written card at least makes me feel that someone was prepared to write a card, add some comments, address the envelope, put a stamp on it and put it in a post box. That's a lot of work!

Direct mail can also offer you more scope for creativity, and you can develop some interesting ideas to grab attention, for example;

- A high quality invitation to an exclusive event;

- A personalised letter of introduction;

- A product sample;

- A branded item or gift;

If you do send direct mail, make sure every piece is personal and addressed to a specific individual.

If you want to send something to the CEO but you don't have a name, do your research and find it.

One word of caution though. We live in a security conscious world, and unsolicited packages can be a problem in some countries.

Whatever you send must be relevant, create interest, grab attention and have a clear call to action. You could ask them to return a pre-paid post card, log onto a website to claim a prize or send an R.S.V.P or email to accept an invitation. You could also tell them to expect a call from you on a predetermined day.

Key points to remember;

- Send pieces in a batch that can be easily followed up;

- Always sign by hand, do not use digitised signatures or have someone sign on your behalf.

- Consider hand-writing the envelope and attaching a postage stamp, because this can be more successful than obviously mass produced mail-shots.

6. EVENTS

Let's talk about those exhibitions, conferences, seminars and events where you get out and meet people.

Exhibitions can be very effective because you can connect with a large number of people in one place, over a relatively short time period.

But they can be expensive, so in this section I'm going to suggest how you can get the best possible return on your investment.

Before you dive into committing a lot of time, effort and money into an event, you should think carefully about the real value to you.

Here are some simple questions that will help you to make an informed decision.

- What's the event about?
- What's the title and theme?
- Who is it targeted at?
- What's the typical attendee profile?

- Is it a generic or niche event?

    Generic covers an industry or generic topic (e.g. Manufacturing) and it will contain a wide range of different products and services. Because of this, not everyone who attends will be interested in what you do.

    Niche focusses on specific segments and topics. This will probably attract less visitors than generic events, but the visitors are more likely to be more relevant for you.

    Obviously the closer the fit between what you do and the visitor's interests, the more enquiries you'll generate.

- What's the agenda?

    Is it strong enough to attract the type of visitor you want to meet?

    Are there prominent speakers?

- Has it been run before?

    How many exhibitors and visitors attended over the last few years?

    Is the event successful and growing or is it in decline?

- Is this a new event?

  What are the organisers doing to attract visitors?
  How will they promote your attendance ?

- How many of your competitors attended?

  If none were there why was that? Did they miss it because they didn't know about it, or did they decide not to attend?

Does it make financial sense?

Value for money is a huge concern because events can be very expensive. That's why you must be brutally honest when you look at return on investment (ROI).

I've seen businesses attend expensive events and come away with few if any quality enquiries.

The result is Zero ROI.

Some marketing people may say it was 'great exposure' and all part of the 'awareness and brand building exercise.' Whilst that may be true in the longer run, the only real metrics that matter are;

- The number of well qualified enquiries;

- How many converted to a sale.

Good measure of success is to look at cost per enquiry. You could also look at the sales revenue generated but unless the sale closes at the event or soon afterwards, there may be further costs involved in selling to the prospect.

Cost per enquiry (CPE) is the number of enquiries divided by the total cost of attending.

Total cost should cover everything including hire of space, accommodation and travel, the cost of having people work your stand and any other ancillary costs.

So if an event costs £10,000 and you get 50 enquiries the CPE is £200. Whether £200 per enquiry is good value is a judgement you will make.

Something to think about is also the average sale price (ASP) of your product. If the ASP is £1,000, you need 10 sales to cover your costs.

You can use this calculation after the event to measure success or you can use it to set some goals such as the number of enquiries you need from the event. This adds extra focus to make sure you engage with visitors, and really put the effort into finding good sales enquiries.

Behaviour

Attending an event is, for some people, an excuse to stay in a hotel, eat and drink to excess, and start each day nursing a hangover.

But that's not how it should be!

I've attended too many events over the years where this has happened. This is not a party, it's a primary selling event.

Your business is on show and for it to project the right image, there are some basic rules that must be followed.

It's a great idea to develop briefing notes for the people on your stand.

It's an even better idea to hold training before the event to ensure everyone is confident and able to deliver the right experience to visitors.

Your people must be able to engage visitors in intelligent conversation and ask the right questions to recognise a sales opportunity.

They must also spend their time with the right people. This means recognising time wasters and dispensing with them as quickly and politely as possible.

Obviously they should always be alert, attentive, polite and professional.

And there are some things they should never do.

- No eating on the stand;
  This not only looks bad, it also creates a mess;

- No slouching, sitting or blocking entry to the stand;
  This almost dares people to dare enter;

- No talking on the phone, amongst themselves, playing with devices or even sending email when visitors are on the stand;
  This indicates that other things are more interesting and important than the visitor;

- No ignoring people who visit the stand:
  It's a fine line between jumping on anyone who steps onto your stand and ignoring them. Let them settle, look around and then approach and ask them how you can help.

After the event

The key to success for any event is to follow up quickly and professionally.

Visitors will talk to many different companies at events, so you must get in fast. The longer you leave it the more likely they are to forget you. That's why you must make an impression when you meet them.

If they are interested, it's best to set up a call or meeting at the event.

If that isn't possible, make sure you contact them soon afterwards by personalised email and then phone call.

Your job then is to qualify if they are a potential client.

If they are not yet ready to engage, nurture them and make regular, relevant contact to engage when the time is right.

If they are ready to engage, you should start the conversation and develop the relationship.

7. NETWORKING

Networking events have become very popular in recent years. They can be a great way of increasing your visibility and broadening your network. A good way to think about them is as part-business, part-social events

But 'networking' is a word that can strike fear into many people's hearts! That's because they are not sure how to go about it. They have questions like;

What do you say when you meet someone?

How should you start the conversation?

How do you end it?

In this section I'm going to give you simple guidelines on how you can get the best results whenever you attend any networking event.

Networking events are about business in a social context. This can sometimes feel awkward, but remember that the people you meet will probably have the same thoughts and fears that you have.

We all know that people prefer to do business with those they like. That's why you should try to relax and let your true personality shine through. Here are a few ideas you can use to get the most out of any networking event.

Create a Power summary

You will remember this from the section on messages and it's the perfect response to the question *"What do you do?"*

You may decide to modify it slightly to suit a particular event, but you should use it to focus on the potential needs of the people you meet, rather than purely promoting yourself.

As Dale Carnegie, author of *'How to win friends and influence people'* said;

> "You can make more friends in two months by becoming interested in other people, than you can in two years by trying to get people interested in you."

Although he wrote that more than half a century ago, the advice is probably even more relevant today with such massive competition for our attention.

Being relevant and meaningful in business is what attracts people to you. And this is a great staring point for any conversation.

Have an objective

The reason many people dislike networking events is because they either hate, or are not good at making small talk. Having a clear objective can help you to overcome this.

That's why it's always a good idea to be very clear about the following;

- Why you are going;

- What you can contribute by being there;

- What you want to achieve;

Create a mini agenda

It's a good idea to have a format to follow. If you don't, it's easy to ramble on and bore someone.

At these events people want to meet others they think will be of use to them. That's why you must establish areas of mutual interest as fast as possible.

Here's an outline I've used many times, that works well. Obviously you use this in a conversational way, rather than just firing questions.

> "Hello, I'm John, it's nice to meet you. It's my first time here, what about you?
>
> What do you do ... where are you based ... how's business?
>
> What are the main things you're interested in? That's interesting, I have a partner /colleague / contact who does that etc ..."

As you can see, these approaches are designed to engage the other person in conversation. And as you now know, that's the best way of establishing rapport and finding areas of common interest.

Close and move on

Don't monopolise one person and remember that like you, they want to meet others.

When you're talking with someone, always give them your undivided attention.

There's nothing worse than someone looking over your shoulder to try to find someone more interesting to talk to. This is just plain bad manners.

When you think you've achieved what you want, or the conversation has reached a natural break point, summarise any agreed actions and move on.

Think on your feet.

It's good to have a clear objective, but you should always stay alert and be open minded.

Opportunities may arise you hadn't thought of. If they do, react to them or if you think they have value, schedule a follow up to go into more depth at a later time.

And finally, these events can sometimes be fun so try to enjoy yourself and who knows, as well as expanding your network, you may also make new friends!

SECTION THREE
Relationships

HOW TO BUILD A SALES MACHINE TO DRIVE GROWTH

Although it takes more than sales skills to succeed, they are a key component in developing strong and sustainable growth.

Selling creates wealth and without it companies and economies have no future.

Selling is in fact, one of the oldest human activities. It created revolutions, built empires and spawned great dynasties.

In this section I'm going to describe the different types of selling. I'll also look at the key qualities a great salesperson must have.

Then I'll talk about a proven sales methodology called Navigator. This has been developed from my more than 30 years of sales experience. It worked very well for me and it can do exactly the same for you.

I'll also talk about presentation skills, which is a mandatory communication skill you must possess.

And at the end there's a worksheet you can use to create your own strategy and put the ideas into immediate use.

SELLING DEFINED

Every great idea and invention needed someone to sell it;

- Ford had Henry Ford;
- Apple had Steve Jobs;
- Virgin has Richard Branson;
- Amazon has Jeff Bezos.

Maybe you don't think of these people as salesmen but they are! They may be founders and CEO's, but they are without doubt, excellent salespeople. They sell their company to many different audiences in many different ways.

Selling isn't about pushing a product or service, it's about solving problems. That's why the best salespeople are seen as problem solvers, trusted advisors who can be relied upon to give great advice.

So selling is the process of satisfying a buyer's wants, needs and desires.

And the best way to do this, is to understand needs and motivation to buy, before you try to sell your product.

Some people believe that a great product sells itself but if that's true, it's because it satisfies a need. Products or services that don't satisfy a need will fail.

In 1985, British inventor Sir Clive Sinclair launched a three wheel battery-assisted vehicle called C5.

It became an object of ridicule and it was a commercial disaster because;

- It had design and production faults;
- It wasn't suited to the British climate;
- It was poorly designed;

A big reason for its failure was because Sir Clive was an inventor not a salesman.

Reinventing the Sale

C5 flopped because it didn't really solve any particular problem. It also failed to capture the imagination because it didn't look very good. In short, C5 just wasn't 'cool'.

Steve Jobs was cool and he was a brilliant salesman.

When Steve announced iPod in 2001 the result was dramatically different, because it solved a problem.

Before iPod you had a portable Compact Disk player. This worked well but you had to carry disks with you and this was sometimes inconvenient. With iPod you could could carry more than 1,000 songs or the equivalent of 100 Compact Disks in your pocket! This revolutionised listening to music as you moved around.

Even the most iconic and desirable products are advertised, promoted and sold, because there's always a choice.

The choice could be to buy another product, or to buy nothing. In fact, 'no decision' (or inertia) can often be the greatest competitor of all.

Before we go much further though, let's look at the different types of selling.

Selling to consumers in a retail environment is different in many ways to selling to professional buyers in a business. These are commonly called business-to-consumer or B2C and business-to-business or B2B.

Lets look at this in the context of selling a cup of coffee and selling an aeroplane.

These icons represent six key areas that illustrate the differences. They are, from left to right;

- Buyers;

- Need or demand;

- Buying process;

- The time it takes to buy;

- Value of the purchase;

- Knowledge required to complete the sale.

One person buys a cup of coffee but for more complicated products many people are involved. Each will have an opinion and you must understand this before you can close a sale. This is sometimes called a complex sale. In fact, mapping all the buyers and influencers in a complex sale is one of the most challenging things to do.

The need in the coffee example is simple and obvious. I buy a coffee because I want to satisfy my caffeine habit! It's an impulse and habitual purchase millions of people make many times a day.

For more complicated products defining the need is harder. It could be to reduce cost, improve efficiency or save a business from failure.

The buying process for coffee is simple and quick. I pick my coffee of choice from the menu and it's produced for me while I wait.

The more complicated a product is, the harder it becomes to make a decision. There will also be more steps involved in the process as we'll see later.

Selling some products takes longer than others because there's more to explain about how it works and what the benefits are. It takes a few minutes to sell a coffee. It can take many months or years to sell aircraft.

Coffee is cheaper than an aeroplane. There's less focus on mitigating risk and no-one cares much if they buy a bad cup of coffee. They'll just go somewhere else next time.

But for a big corporate procurement, there's far more at stake. Getting this wrong can wreck careers.

If I'm a Barista I know the difference between a Cappuccino and an Espresso.

But the more complicated a product is, the more you need to know about how it works, and how it benefits the buyer.

The point to all of this is that you need a sales approach that works for whatever it is that you sell. And then there are three things you really must focus on;

1. Providing a different (unique) buying experience;

2. Delivering great service;

3. Creating buyer preference and loyalty.

There are many coffee shops, but Starbucks set out to create something different. They called it a 'third place', somewhere between home and work where people could read, relax, meet friends and drink coffee.

Other coffee chains have tried to create their own versions, but *'going for a Starbucks'* has entered the lexicon as meaning *'let's get coffee'*.

Starbucks say they have special blends of coffee. But can anyone really pick a Starbucks from a Caffe Nero or Coffee Republic blend in a blind test?

Maybe some people can, but the vast majority of us use a particular brand, because of the experience we get. And when you have a favourite, you generally go back, time and time again.

So now you know why B2C selling is different to and similar in some ways to B2B. Let's now look at what makes a great salesperson.

TOP PERFORMERS

I'm frequently asked two questions;

1. What does it take to be a top sales performer?

2. Can anyone become good at sales?

These are good questions because there's a common misconception that great salespeople are born, blessed with natural talents and the right personality.

They are great talkers and they can sell anything because they have the "Sales Gene!"

There may be some truth in this, because personality obviously plays a part. But being successful requires more than a pleasing demeanour, a great line in chat and a nice smile.

Anyone can become a top performer but it takes intelligence, work and commitment. It's not just a case of learning a sales pitch and talking to as many prospective buyers as you can.

Top performers are seen by their clients as experts in their field, trusted advisors who can solve a problem.

But this isn't achieved by luck, because top performers work hard to perfect their craft.

Over the years I've interviewed, hired, trained and managed hundreds of sales professionals, so I know what it takes to be a top performer.

These icons illustrate the 6 key skills needed. They are, from left to right;

1. Great communicator;

2. Ability to understand buyers motivation;

3. Domain expert;

4. Strategic thinker;

5. Possess the right attitude;

6. Organised and work efficiently.

Great communicator

Sales is about uncovering needs and communicating your value to buyers. It's not about pitching a product hard at someone and hoping they will buy.

It's about building relationships based on trust, rather than purely promoting self-interest.

The key to uncovering needs is to ask questions, and engage people in conversation. Information is then shared in a way that's clear, concise and compelling. Their presentations are always engaging and they have an ability to establish rapport and build trust.

Understand buyer motivation

Top performers are well informed and they really understand the challenges buyers face.

They know what's going on in their industry and they clearly understand what motivates people to buy.

Domain expert

Top performers know their products inside out and are acknowledged experts in their field. They can clearly describe how their products will solve the buyer's problems better than the alternatives.

Strategic thinker

Top performers know how to plan successful sales campaigns that achieve results as efficiently as possible. This minimises the cost of sale and lays the foundations of a long-term relationship.

They see the big picture and regard a sale as the start of a relationship, rather than the end. Their goal is to drive repeat business, obtain referrals and build buyer loyalty.

The right attitude

Top performers are confident because they're good. They have a positive mental attitude which means they always look for the upside in any situation. They focus on what they can do, rather than on what they can't.

They see obstacles and problems as challenges to be overcome. They combine this with intuition and judgement to avoid chasing opportunities they can't win or shouldn't bid for.

As well as having the right attitude, top performers are honest which is why people regard them as a trusted advisor, rather than a purely self-interested salesperson.

Organised

Top performers know that sales success doesn't happen by accident. That's why they use a sales process.

They know that by working in a structured way, they focus on the important things they must do to win business, and build relationships. This helps them to win most of the business they bid on.

BUYING AND SELLING

Buying and selling are mirror images of each other and I'm going to show how you can bring them together, in a way that dramatically improves your performance.

HOW BUYERS SEE THE WORLD

When a business makes a purchase it will usually follow a buying process. How complicated this is, will depend on the business and what they are buying.

There's clearly a lot more involved in buying a very expensive item of capital equipment, than there is buying office supplies.

The more you understand about how this works, the better your chances of success.

Although this will vary, the following steps are pretty common.

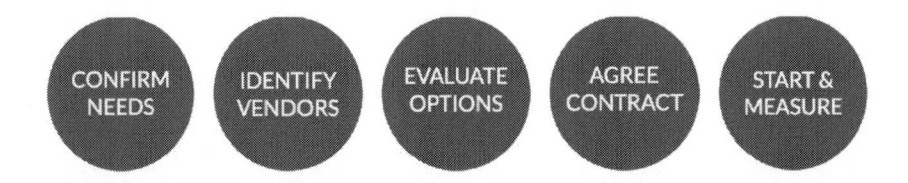

CONFIRM NEEDS → IDENTIFY VENDORS → EVALUATE OPTIONS → AGREE CONTRACT → START & MEASURE

Confirm needs

This is where they define exactly what they are looking for. They could give you a general description or formal documents such as the following;

> Pre-qualification questionnaire (PQQ) or Request for information (RFI);
> *A screening document to develop a short-list of potential suppliers;*

> Invitation to tender (ITT), Request for quotation (RFQ) or Request for proposal (RFP);
> A *detailed statement of requirements that short-listed suppliers are asked to complete.*

Identify vendors

Some organisations may already have a list of approved suppliers. However as things change, they may monitor the market and evaluate new suppliers.

They will draw up a long list of potential suppliers who seem to have the right skills and track record. These are contacted or sent the PQQ or RFI and the short-list is created.

They'll then use scoring criteria and send the ITT, RFQ or RFP to the short-list.

Evaluate options

As part of the evaluation process, each supplier is normally asked to present their proposal.

They may also be asked to provide information through a combination of workshops, presentations, demonstrations and reference visits.

Based on this, a decision is made on a preferred supplier.

Agree contract

Buyers will sometimes negotiate with one or more suppliers to get the best agreement.

Start and measure

Once a contract has been signed, the product or service is delivered and progress is evaluated to ensure it conforms with the specification.

HOW SALESPEOPLE SEE THE WORLD

Whereas a buying process will vary, I'd expect to see all these steps being covered in most sales situations.

FIND LEADS → QUALIFY POTENTIAL → DELIVER PROPOSAL → SELL & CLOSE → CREATE ADVOCATE

Find leads

The staring point for every sale is obviously finding people to sell to.

Qualify potential

Qualification is where you ask basic questions to discover if a sales lead is worth pursuing.

Deliver proposal

This is where you respond to their statement of needs (ITT / RFQ / RFP) or you make an outline proposal to start the conversation.

Sell and close

You present your ideas, go into more detail and keep qualifying to make sure you are on track to win.

This is where negotiations take place to agree the exact terms and conditions. If it all goes according to plan you sign a contract.

Create advocate

A signed contract is the start of the relationship. The focus should the switch to deliver excellent service to develop a happy and satisfied client.

You'll notice that these typical buying and sales processes are similar in many ways.

CONFIRM NEEDS	IDENTIFY VENDORS	EVALUATE OPTIONS	AGREE CONTRACT	START & MEASURE
FIND LEADS	QUALIFY POTENTIAL	DELIVER PROPOSAL	SELL & CLOSE	CREATE ADVOCATE

As I said earlier, they are different sides of the same activity. That's why it's so important to understand how people buy. And the best way to do this is to work in a structured way to get the information you need.

If you remember what I said earlier, this is one of the key qualities all top performers possess.

They follow a sales process that helps them understand how people buy. Then they plan a sales campaign to maximise the chances of success.

Before I talk about sales process though, I'm going to talk about why you need to use a process, and the benefits this will give you.

BENEFITS OF USING A SALES PROCESS

Maximise sales opportunity

By understanding more about the way people buy, you focus on opportunities you can win.

Improve efficiency and reduce the cost of sale

Selling is a tough job but a sales process makes it easier. It helps you to minimise unproductive activities and focus on the priorities. This eliminates wasted effort and results in a more cost efficient and profitable sales operation.

Provide a solid platform for predictable growth

Because you qualify every sales opportunity, you get more clarity on which sales are most likely to close. This means you can make more accurate sales forecasts, which gives you a solid base for planning the growth of your business.

Drive competitive advantage

Working in a structured way projects a professional image because you focus on understanding needs, solving problems and developing a relationship.

This differentiates you from competitors who just push their product, and try everything to close a sale.

I've used many different sales processes over the years. The problem is that some were just too simplistic and others far too complicated.

So I decided to create something new.

Something that made perfect sense.

Something that's relatively simple, easy to follow and covers all the key areas.

My process is called Navigator and that's what the rest of this section describes in some depth.

NAVIGATOR SALES PROCESS

Navigator is based on techniques I've used over many years to sell hundreds of millions of pounds worth of information technology and related products and services.

I know from experience that you can waste a lot of time and money trying to sell to someone who is either not ready, or able to buy. And that's where Navigator helps. It'll guide you through a sales campaign, using core sales skills to perform key actions that help you win. Navigator has four stages each of which incorporates best practice sales techniques.

1. **Screen** is a high level initial qualification stage to decide if you should work on an opportunity.

2. If you decide there is an opportunity, you move to the second phase called **Plan**. This is where you qualify more deeply and develop a plan to win.

3. **Engage** is the active selling phase where you present your product or service and sell the benefits. In this phase you'll be developing the relationship, building trust and giving the buyer confidence in your ability to deliver. You will of course also still be qualifying to make sure you're on track to win.

4. When you've won the business you move into the fourth phase which is called **Develop**. Here you focus on providing exceptional service and creating an advocate.

Advocates are very important because they not only buy again, they also act as a reference and will give you referrals.

Although Navigator has four stages, please don't think you have to work through them sequentially. Maybe that works in a perfect world, but none of us work there!

You will find that in some cases you flip between the first three stages. That's normal and I'll explain how that can happen as I go through the next few sections.

So let's look at how you can use Navigator to achieve the very best sales results.

STAGE ONE - SCREEN

When you get a sales lead you must screen it. This is important because you want to use your time wisely by working with people who are likely to buy.

This is the most basic rule of successful sales. If you talk with the right people, you'll sell more.

And you can find out if they are the 'right' people by doing some basic research online.

You can of course check them out on Google and sites like LinkedIn, Facebook, and Twitter.

This information will help you to build up a personal picture of who they are, what they do and possibly what their views are on certain topics.

Then, when you call them you can ask relevant and intelligent questions to get the conversation started.

To screen them properly you will want to know some or all of the following;

- What are they trying to achieve?
- What are they looking for?
- What options are they considering?
- What stage are they at in the buying cycle?
- When do they want to make a decision?
- What's driving this timescale?
- Do they have a budget or an expectation of cost?

These are important questions because your chances of success are increased when;

- You understand their motivation to buy;
- You know you have a viable solution;
- There's commitment and urgency to make a decision.

And we all know that no urgency generally means there's no motivation to buy now.

If this opportunity doesn't pass the screen, you may decide to either drop them or stay in touch and follow up later.

If you decide there is an immediate opportunity, you'll want to spend time getting to know more. You can of course do research, but the best way I know to learn more is to ask questions.

The ability to ask relevant and intelligent questions is a core sales skill you must master.

The importance of questions

Communication is a 2 way process and top performers know this. Instead of pushing their product or service, they ask questions to discover people's wants, needs and motivation to buy.

Top performers ask questions and share information all the way through a sale. They do this to make sure that they understand the buyer's needs, because this helps them to position their offering in the best way.

By doing this they also build trust, which is a big factor in winning business. A buyer who likes and trusts you, is far more likely to do business with you. That's just a fact of human nature.

Top performers ask great questions because they think clearly about what they need to know. They plan their questions and create a list. This is really easy if you start with some simple headings like;

- What … do you want to achieve?
- Why … do you want to do something?
- Who … else is involved in making a decision?
- When … do you want to make a decision?
- How … do you make a decision?

These are great lead-ins to frame many different questions. Use them and you'll see an immediate improvement in the way you build rapport with your prospects.

Top performers are also great listeners.

When they've asked a question they shut up and listen carefully to the answer. Then they follow up with another question or comment, or they give information that prompts a question.

And that's how a business conversation develops.

The buyer will decide if you're the kind of person they want to do business with. And you'll be able to decide if this is a good business opportunity you can win.

There are two basic types of question that you can use to develop a conversational flow - Open and Closed.

> Open questions can't be answered with a straight yes or no. They require more explanation which provides information you can use to expand the conversation.

> Closed questions are normally answered with a yes, no or confirmation of some fact. These are useful because they provide a contrast and they take less thought and effort to answer.

When you mix your open and closed questions, you can create a natural conversation flow that works really well.

So if you think about your questions in advance, you won't miss the information you need or wonder what to say next.

One last thing, always be polite and say please and thank you. This is basic good manners, it costs nothing and it really does help to build a relationship based on mutual respect.

STAGE TWO - PLAN

If an opportunity looks promising you'll be keen to make progress. And the best way to do this, is to create a plan to help you close the sale.

But for many businesses, this is where the problem starts.

Some create complex plans that contain too much information. These are hard to work through and it's almost impossible to focus on the key areas.

Others have no plan at all. At the first sniff of a sales opportunity, they dive into a presentation or demonstration and hope that their brilliant product will dazzle the buyer into saying yes.

And sometimes that does happen if you've got a cool new piece of consumer electronics. But if you're selling to a business it normally makes sense to have a plan.

As I said earlier, people buy to solve a problem or satisfy a need. The purpose of a plan is to understand that motivation and then work in a structured way to satisfy it.

Your plan should be as simple as possible and cover the following four key areas;

1. What they do

This describes their business and the way they make money. It's important you understand this because the more you know about their business, the better you'll be able to help them.

2. Why they want to buy

This describes the reason they want to buy. And the more you understand about this, the better you can solve their problem.

3. Who is involved in buying

You must know who is directly and indirectly involved in making a decision to buy because you must convince them that you have the best solution.

4. Why they should buy from you

Make it easy for them to select you by describing clearly why you are the best choice for them.

Navigator sales plan has 6 sections that will help you to compile the information you need;

The Profile tab contains the basic static information about the prospect and their business.

The Problem tab is where you confirm why they want to buy. On this and every other page, you'll notice a 'What don't we know' box. This is useful because as you go through the process of qualifying a sales opportunity, there will be missing information.

Navigator Sales Plan

PROFILE

Organization		Location	
Project		Reason	
Primary Contact		Timescale	
Source		Value	

PROBLEM

Pain/Opportunity?		Impact ?	
ROI?		Urgency?	
Compelling Event?		What don't we know?	

Your goal should be to get what you need to make sure the sale is on track. But don't become too obsessed with this because in many cases you will have to work with incomplete information.

You'll then have to make decisions based on what you've learned and can deduce. This judgement will develop as your skills improve.

The People tab is pretty self-explanatory. It's where you gather information on those involved in the sale, so you can decide how you need to work with them.

Navigator Sales Plan

PEOPLE

Who is involved?		Previous experience of similar projects?	
Who has the most Power and Influence?		Have we met who we need to?	
Who has final sign off?		Outside influences - technology partners, consultants?	
What relationships do we have?		Who wants us to win? - Why?	
Who do we need to cultivate?		What don't we know?	

The Position tab is slightly more subjective, and it's a way of building a picture of your position relative to the competition.

POSITION — **Navigator Sales Plan**

		Name	Role	Rating	Mode
+5	Enthusiastic Advocate				
+4	Strongly Supportive				
+3	Supportive				
+2	Interested				
+1	Will go along				
-1	Probably won't resist				
-2	Uninterested				
-3	Mildly Negative				
-4	Strong for Competition				
-5	Antagonistic Anti-Sponsor				
G	Growth				
T	Trouble				
E	Even Keel				

Role means what they do in the organisation e.g. Finance Director, Buyer.

Rating is how you think they view you. There are 10 possible categories to choose from. You could of course simplify this and have just 2 - for and against.

As I said earlier, this is usually a subjective view because you can't always believe what people tell you in business.

I'm not being cynical, just realistic because although some people are truthful, others keep things to themselves or mislead you. Again you'll have to make a judgement based on what people say, and then validate that with other people and through what you learn.

Mode refers to where they are currently - and I've shown 3 modes - Growth, Trouble and Even Keel.

This helps to define motivation so if someone is in Growth mode, it means that they want to exploit opportunities.

If someone is in Trouble mode, they will want to solve a problem.

And when someone is in Even Keel mode, they are probably not highly motivated to do anything!

It's important to understand this because if you can help them grow or avoid trouble, your chances of success are increased. That's why you must present your ideas in a way that aligns with the buyer's basic motivations.

When you pull all this together, you can paint an interesting profile of the people you are dealing with.

The Process tab helps you to understand how decisions are actually made. And this enables you to present your proposal in a way that grabs the maximum attention.

PROCESS	**Navigator Sales Plan**	
Decision Making Criteria?		How - Spec, Fully costed ROI, Workshop, Exec presentation, other?
Political, Social, Economic factors?		Where does funding come from?
How long will this take?		What don't we know?

The Plan tab on the following page, is where you pull everything together into a time-phased set of actions to win the sale.

In summary

There are no hard rules in using this plan other than to make it relevant to what you sell, and to keep it as simple as possible.

I'm not suggesting that you don't actively sell until you've completed a plan because that's just not realistic. Getting the information you need to build your plan can take time.

You may have to get people excited by showing them your product, or pitching ideas. In some cases you'll have to earn their trust before they are even prepared to give you the information you want.

But if you want to be a top performer you must always have a plan. The more you understand, the better your chance of success. It really is that simple.

Navigator Sales Plan

PLAN

What	When	Who	Status

STAGE THREE - ENGAGE

When you engage in a sales campaign you generally have to do 4 things;

> 1. Educate the audience about how your product or service fits their needs;
>
> 2. Prove your capabilities through a presentation, demonstration, workshop, trial or client reference;
>
> 3. Confirm your offer through a formal request for information or tender process;
>
> 4. Agree the terms of a sale agreement;

One of the most critically important skills you must master, is the ability to communicate your ideas to your audience.

Communication covers every aspect of making a sale.

- In a one-on-one meeting;
- In a small group;
- When you present to an audience.

The aim in every situation is to get your message across in the most clear, concise and compelling way possible.

I call these Presentation Skills and because this is such an important topic ,I've devoted a whole section to it later.

Closing the sale

The end objective in every sale is to get the buyer to say yes. This is often called 'closing', and it frightens some people. They feel nervous asking for the order in case the buyer says no and I'll come to how you handle that in a moment.

If the buyer is still committed to buy and you've convinced them that you're the best choice, closing is just the next logical step. But the problems start if you make a big deal out of it, or try to apply too much pressure.

Most buyers today are well informed, pretty sharp and unlikely to be swayed by cheap sales talk. Of course you'll probably have to negotiate and the buyer may ask for a discount or other special terms. But it's the way you respond to this that determines your success.

After all, anyone can give something away or discount the price, because this takes no skill. What does take skill, is to make sure that you and the buyer realise you are trying to reach an agreement that's fair to both parties.

So closing is not one event, it should be the completion of a sequence of events.

It's your job to make sure the buyer understands your proposition and is still interested in doing business with you. And you do this by asking questions and getting feedback all the way through the sales process. You are constantly qualifying and checking to make sure you are on track.

There's nothing wrong with asking someone in a polite yet direct way, if they are ready to place an order. After all, if you've done everything they've asked you to, you've earned that right.

However there are times when your buyer may stop returning your calls, or decide not to go ahead. It could be that they have a better offer, or their need has gone away. This is called an objection and you must handle it in the right way to stand any chance of winning the business.

Handling objections

In any sales situation there are times when things don't go according to plan.

The buyer raises questions, resists your attempts to get them to take some action, make a commitment or buy when you ask them to.

These are typically called objections and the way you handle them is all about your attitude. If you view resistance or reluctance as a big problem or something that will stop the sale, you really should think again.

If you've followed the sales process, qualified the buyer well and things have progressed, an objection can mean a number of things.

1. They are not yet ready to buy because perhaps they need more information or a stronger business case;

2. They think there are better offers from your competitors;

3. The value proposition isn't strong enough. In other words they don't think the price you are asking, reflects what it's worth to them;

4. They don't fully understand what you're offering;

5. They no longer have decision making ability and they want to save face;

6. There's been a change in their priorities and their needs have changed. Perhaps the reason for buying has either gone away, or been solved in some other way;

7. They want a discount.

Maybe you can think of others, but the point is that when someone says 'No' you must find out if it means 'No never, not now or I'm not sure.'

Of course there are many reasons buyers raise objections and some are real, whilst others are hidden. They may not want to tell you what they are for personal and business reasons, but unless you get to the true objection and fully understand it, you won't make progress.

It's very easy to panic or dive in and answer what you think the objection is. It's also easy to offer concessions or drop the price, but this is a very big mistake.

Before you take any action, make sure that you understand the real objection. And you can do that by following a simple 4 step approach;

```
   1            2              3            4
 LISTEN     UNDERSTAND      ANSWER      CONFIRM
```

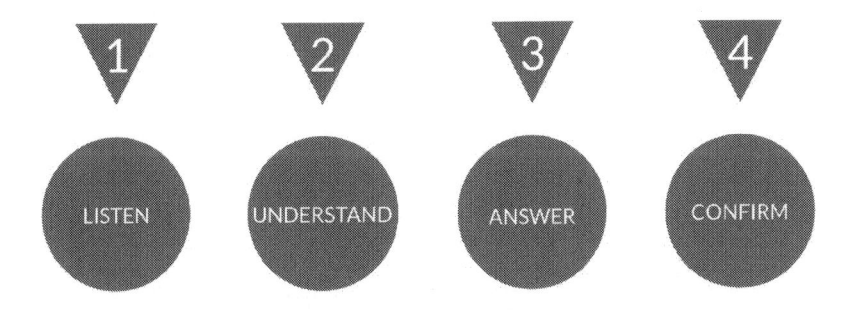

1. Listen very carefully to what they say

Don't make any assumptions, be cool, calm and let them talk. Never interrupt and answer what you think the objection is.

2. Understand their real objection by asking questions such as;

"So are you saying that you think our competitor is 25% cheaper for exactly the same product?"

Don't be in a rush to jump on that one point though. It's best to understand if there are others so you could ask;

"Thanks for that, so as well as price, are there any other issues that are concerning you?"

This is important because if they have other objections, you want to get the whole list so you know exactly what you need to do to move forward.

3. Answer the real objection

Don't think about this as winning an argument, proving the other person is wrong, mistaken or worse still, stupid! Your aim is not to score points, it's to win business. They could be genuinely confused because you haven't given them all the information they need.

Your competitors may also have planted some misleading information about your product. Or they've seen something in your offer that they don't like. Whatever it is, it's your job to get to the bottom of it.

If your competitor really is 25% cheaper, you could match the price, offer other inducements, try to minimise the price difference or pull out.

4. Confirm they understand and accept your answer

After you've given a response, check they understand your answer and accept it. If they do move towards a close. If they don't you must go back and handle it again or decide what action to take next.

If you think you've answered all their questions then you'll probably feel confident you can win the business. The next question is 'when' and this is one of the most important and difficult questions to answer.

SALES FORECASTING

Forecasting the flow of revenue is critically important because you need that visibility to make plans for the future.

But this is an area of weakness in many businesses. There's often a disconnect between the activity of selling, and the preparation of a sales forecast.

This may sound strange but it's true. In many businesses a sales forecast is a guess or even a gamble that things will work out.

Most salespeople are optimistic by nature and they expect the best in every situation. That's obviously a great quality to have, but it must be tempered with a degree of realism.

Some salespeople believe a sales is as good as done at a very early stage. I've heard experienced people say that a deal was 'in the bag' after one meeting!

What's needed is a forecasting process that is simple, easy to understand and reliable. And that's what I've created to help you introduce more certainty into your business.

Here's a suggested approach that links forecasting directly with the stages of the Navigator sales process.

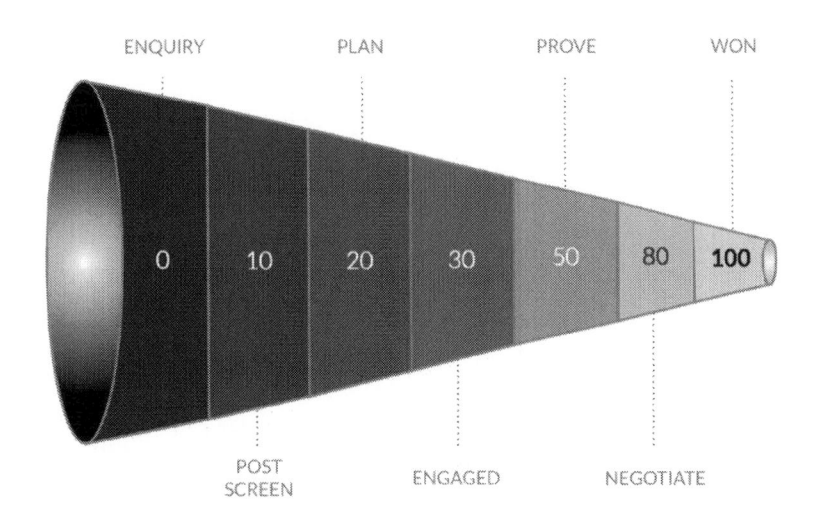

ENQUIRY	PLAN		PROVE		WON
0	10	20	30	50	80	100

POST SCREEN — ENGAGED — NEGOTIATE

The basic idea is that as the opportunity moves through the different stages of the sales process, the probability of winning increases.

Probability is the key factor because this determines the degree of certainty and confidence you attach to winning a sale.

An initial enquiry is rated at zero because it's not yet clear if this really is an opportunity. If there is a potential fit after screening it's shown at 10%.

As you engage in a more detailed discovery it goes up to 20%, reflecting the fact that it's becoming more of a firm opportunity.

When you're actively engaged and building a relationship, the probability increases still further. But as long as there's competition, there's still a threat.

It probably makes sense to be conservative unless you are the preferred and possibly only supplier they are negotiating with.

And because the unexpected can happen, it's only really 'in the bag' when you have a signed contract and payment!

The way you create a forecast is up to you, but it can be a simple spreadsheet with four columns;

Name - Value - Probability - Forecast

- Value is what the sale is worth;

- Probability is percentage based on current position;

- Forecast is value based on probability.

So if your sale has a total value of £100,000 and you're actively engaged, the probability is 30%. This gives you a current forecast value of £30,000.

Even when you're engaged and actively selling, it's only shown at 50% probability. You could of course be more bullish than this, but make sure you take a realistic view and not one based on hearsay or hope.

STAGE FOUR - DEVELOP

This is where you build the relationship and create an advocate.

Some people still believe that the selling ends when someone buys. But that's a big mistake because everyone has choice. There's such intense competition in almost every sector, that your clients will go elsewhere unless you give them reasons to stay with you.

So when you've won a sale, focus on creating advocates who will buy again, endorse your business and give you referrals.

We all know it's much easier and far less expensive to sell to someone you've already done business with. You're now in prime position to create a mutually profitable relationship.

The value to you can extend well beyond the initial transaction though. By listening and learning, you'll be able to harness ideas to;

- Improve existing products or develop new ones;

- Simplify your processes and make it easier for people to do business with you;

- Develop your customer service to create deeper relationships that build trust;

You can get feedback from clients by staying in regular contact with them. But don't just call when you're trying to sell something.

Keep in touch by sending news, information, email, messages or calling them on a fairly regular basis. This is sometimes called 'account management', I call it common sense!

You can get a lot of feedback online. Every day people are writing blogs, using message boards, making comments on websites, updating their Facebook and LinkedIn status and Tweeting their thoughts to the world.

There's a torrent of data swirling around the planet, and some of it is generated by people who are your employees, partners and current or future clients.

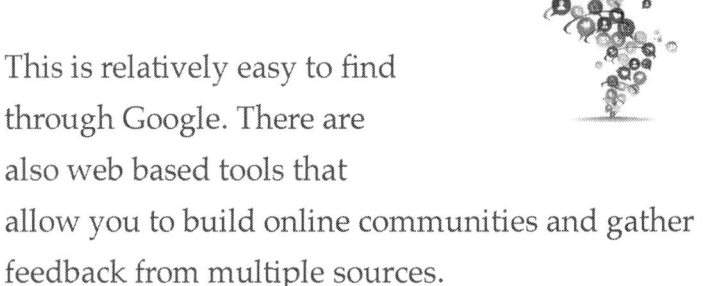

This is relatively easy to find through Google. There are also web based tools that allow you to build online communities and gather feedback from multiple sources.

Here you can see what clients, partners and employees are talking about. You can use this knowledge to measure the effectiveness of communication campaigns, identify business opportunities, assess competitor activity and even give you early warning of potential problems.

And most importantly, you can use it to deliver a better experience for your audience, which in turn drives growth!

PRESENTING YOUR IDEAS

To be a successful salesperson you must be able to share your ideas with an audience. This may seem difficult and daunting, especially if you haven't done much of it before. But don't worry, because it's not really that difficult if you follow my advice.

The key to being a good presenter is to think about it as telling a story. And as you know, the primary purpose of a good story is to grab attention and keep it.

When you've created your story, you will mould it into a format that you can present to your audience. This is called presentation design.

Then you'll present it in a way that will captivate, educate, entertain and change your audience's perspective in some way. This is called presentation delivery.

These are the 2 areas you must master to be a confident, engaging and successful presenter.

PRESENTATION DESIGN

There are 2 key parts to designing your presentation;

1. Writing the story;

2. Creating the slides.

Writing the story

If you've read the section on messages, you'll know that the best messages are clear, concise and compelling. And that's exactly what your story and presentation must be.

Every story needs a plot or Big Idea which is the central theme of your presentation. It describes what it's about, and everything flows from there.

Think about the impact your Big Idea will have on your audience. Will they be mildly intrigued or massively inspired and motivated to take some action? Why is your Big Idea different and why should the audience care?

You must understand who the audience is, what they are interested in and why they are at your presentation.

Your results will be far better when you align the audience's interests and motivation with your Big Idea.

When you're clear about this, you must turn the Big Idea into a powerful but simple title. Make it action oriented so it describes the benefits the audience will get by listening. Titles like 'How to grow revenues by 50%' or 'Messages that never fail' are far more engaging than 'Presentation to, Discussion on or Overview of' types of titles.

When you've nailed the title you can write your story. Write as though you are speaking, because this is the best way to make your story flow naturally. You can use whatever writing tools you prefer, but always follow this basic flow;

Introduction

Summarise your Big Idea and why you believe the audience should care. Then you should give a high level summary of all the areas you will cover. This is the flow of your presentation which could include your list of topics or agenda.

Detail

Here you will drill down into appropriate detail on key areas. This is where you can demonstrate your expertise by talking about key issues and if appropriate how you address them.

Summary

This is where you bring everything together. You will reiterate your Big Idea, summarise key points and close on whatever commitment you're looking for.

When you've done this you will have what looks like a speech. Next, edit it to take out any padding or useless words. Then break the story up into slide-sized chunks. These will be your presenter notes from which you can create each slide.

I'm not suggesting that you learn your presentation by heart, but the very act of writing and splitting it in this way will load it into your memory. This will make you far more confident, relaxed and able to demonstrate your expertise.

When you're happy with your story and the flow, it's time to turn your attention to designing each slide.

SLIDE DESIGN

Design is more than choosing a template, colour scheme or font. It's not just about style, it's about providing a better user experience which makes it easier for the audience to understand your story and get excited by it.

If you've ever suffered from 'Death by Powerpoint', you'll know that it's not much fun.

You sit there bored out of your mind as the clock seems to simply drag by. You're thinking about anything other than what's being said. You zone out and start doodling, or checking Facebook or email. In fact, you're probably doing anything except listening to the presenter drone on and on. You just want it to end.

So the last thing you want to become is a 'Death by Powerpoint' kind of presenter. And if you follow my advice, I promise that will never happen.

Of course I can't absolutely guarantee that you'll become a 'rock star' presenter overnight. But I can guarantee that if you follow these simple rules, you'll take major steps in that direction.

This advice is based on my own personal experience of delivering hundreds of presentations over many years, so I've learned what works and what doesn't. I'm helping you to avoid some of the harsh learning experiences I've had!

If you focus on 6 key areas, you will see an instant improvement in the quality of your presentation design.

1. Simplicity

Simplicity is the essence of clear communication. This is obvious because the simpler something is to grasp, the faster you understand it.

But simplicity doesn't mean 'dumbing down' and losing valuable content just to be brief. It means distilling your story to the absolute core by removing anything that doesn't help understanding.

The ability to say more with less is a skill you must develop. And the more you understand your subject, the easier this will be.

A good way to do this is to look at each slide in your presentation, and ask yourself 4 questions;

1. What's the purpose of this slide?

2. What message or idea do I want to get across?

3. How can I make the point with fewer (or no) words?

4. Is there a stunning image I can use that sums it up?

Be careful not to overdo it though, because you must find the right balance and this depends on your message, the audience and the purpose of the presentation.

A complex technical subject will obviously require some detail, but avoid padding because this leads to information overload even for the brightest people!

I'm often asked 'How many ideas should I put on a slide?'

The answer is ONE.

This is backed by cognitive research, which proves that when you give someone information in easily digestible chunks, their retention and recall is vastly improved.

2. Clutter

Clutter is anything that doesn't add value or make it easier to understand the message. The biggest culprits are things like company logos, slogans and copyright notices.

These are annoying and they cut down on the available space you can use for the really interesting stuff. Unfortunately this is common practice, but what do these actually add? And how do they help the audience get excited about your message?

Keep the slides free for the really important things you want the audience to remember, and only show your company name and logo on the first and last slide. culprits are things like company logos, slogans and copyright notices.

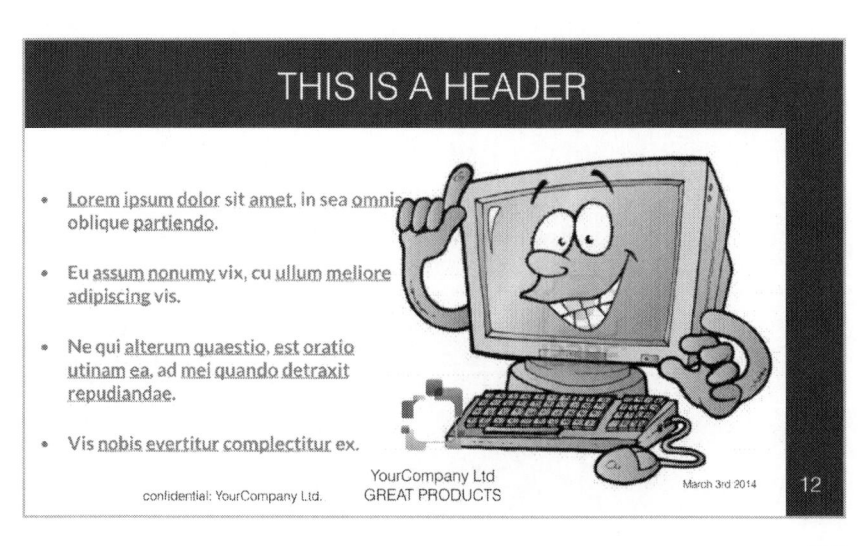

These are annoying and they cut down on the available space you can use for the really interesting stuff.

Unfortunately this is common practice, but what do these actually add? And how do they help the audience get excited about your message?

Keep the slides free for the really important things you want the audience to remember, and only show your company name and logo on the first and last slide.

3. Words

A presentation should be mainly visual. If it's crammed with words it's a report and you should hand it over for the audience to read.

But the main reason people ignore this and cram text onto a slide is because they don't really know the story. Or they don't know how to present information in the right way.

The most common way people use text is with the dreaded bullet point. You see them everywhere, because people fire up their presentation software and just enter text. This is their idea of developing a presentation and it's sloppy, unprofessional, lazy and the major cause of 'Death by Powerpoint.'

Your presentation should be like a film documentary that tells a story with images and the spoken word.

If you think in this way, you won't need a lot of text or bullet points on every slide. With words, less is definitely more because the words you use must have impact and meaning.

4. Images

Many studies have shown that a powerful image can make a far bigger, and more lasting impact than words alone. And the more relevant and concrete the image is, the more powerful the effect. That's why an image should not just be decorative. It must be a visual metaphor which makes a point.

Never use cheap or free clip art images because they look unprofessional and bad.

Always use high quality images, even if you have to buy them.

You can get some good free high resolution images but it's also worth looking at some of the better stock image sites such as Fotolia, iStockphoto and Shutterstock. You'll find images are surprisingly affordable, and all the sites offer monthly subscription packages that provide excellent value for money.

5. Composition

Composition describes the way you place your content on a slide to maximise the impact.

A good way to do this is to think like a photographer, designer or artist. They use various techniques for framing their subjects to make them more interesting. One good technique is called the Rule of Thirds.

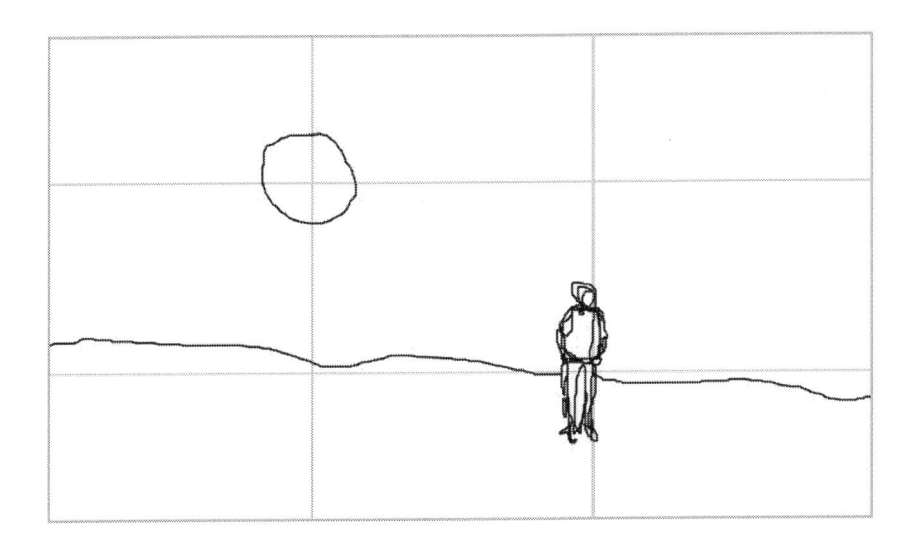

The basic idea is to break a slide into a 3 x 3 block grid, and then place the subject at key points of interest, rather than the default setting of dead centre. You could place the image top right, bottom left, filling a slide or even bleeding over an edge. There's no right answer on composition, so experiment and see what you think looks best.

'White space' is another compositional technique that works very well.

It isolates and frames a word, phrase or image for maximum impact. This is very effective at focussing attention and it can also look elegant and sophisticated.

As well as using space to isolate and frame something, you should also consider the space between related items. Make sure it's obvious which image and item of text go together, so they are viewed as a group rather than random elements on a slide.

There is no right or wrong answer on composition, other than making it easy for the audience to know where you want them to focus their attention.image for maximum impact.

6. Effects

Some people get so excited about the special effects and sounds they can add with Powerpoint, Keynote and other presentation software.

But unless these are used wisely, you can end up with something that's close to sensory overload as objects slide in on a comet flash and slides explode from one to the other.

I'm sure you've seen this many times, and the novelty wears off very fast.

Simplicity dictates that you don't complicate things by adding distracting clutter. And special effects can be a major cause of clutter.

Before you go live with any special effects, ask yourself how they make it easier for the audience to understand your story. Your job is not to show how much you know about adding special effects, it's to get the audience excited about your Big Idea.

PRESENTATION DELIVERY

We often hear people say that truly great communicators are born. When we think about Martin Luther King, Nelson Mandela, John F Kennedy, and Steve Jobs, we see natural performers who could captivate an audience. Of course they were naturally gifted people, but were they born with a skill to communicate, or did they learn?

Some people do have a natural skill, but the truly inspired communicators have an attention to detail and a total commitment to getting it right.

Former Apple CEO and founder Steve Jobs was truly obsessive, and his legendary drive for delivering the perfect presentation drove his people crazy.

He would fuss over the most minute detail and would work himself hard to make sure that everything was just right. When showtime arrived, he was all California cool, relaxed and talking to the audience as though they were having a chat over coffee.

There are many great examples of Steve's presentations online, and it's worth spending a little time looking at a true master at work.

Although not everyone can join this band of iconic communicators, you can improve dramatically if you follow some basic advice.

The most important thing to remember is that you're the star. The slides you've created are just the props you'll use to tell your story. You are the essential ingredient that makes the whole thing come alive.

To perform at your best, you should master these 4 things;

1. Attitude

The audience takes it cue from you, so you must be positive and enthusiastic about your topic. You must convey your sheer delight and excitement about being in front of them sharing your Big Idea.

Genuine enthusiasm is infectious. It makes you stand out and it's hard not to like someone who is personable, well informed and entertaining. When you create the right environment, you will make an immediate connection with the audience. This is very important because when they like you, they'll be more inclined to give you a fair hearing. They'll even be keen for you to succeed.

2. Pace

Striking the right pace is really important. Great communicators seem relaxed and comfortable. They act and speak in a measured and controlled way. They don't gabble or speak at a million miles an hour. You can understand every word they say, and you follow the story easily.

Look at some of the best at work by attending live events or viewing videos online. It's fine to model yourself on someone you admire, but add in your own personal touches to create a unique style that works for you.

3. Knowledge

Knowing your stuff is mandatory. You're the one standing up addressing the room so they expect you to know what you're talking about, it's that simple.

Need I really say more?

4. Timing

Making a presentation the right length is important to avoid Death by Powerpoint.

Remember when I spoke about attention spans earlier? You must make your presentation as long as it needs to be and no longer. It's fine to set the scene and establish rapport, in fact that's an essential part of creating a positive environment. But avoid the padding and small-talk that no-one really wants to hear.

Studies have shown that concentration levels dip after 15 minutes. I know that this is less for many senior people, so keep these simple points in mind and you'll be fine;

1. Get to the point as fast as possible;

2. Don't cram too much in;

3. Always try to finish early.

Rehearsals

It's such an old cliche, but practice really does make perfect. That's why it's always a good idea to run through your presentation a few times, either on your own or with a group of colleagues.

It's very easy to rehearse on your own anytime, anywhere. You just run through the presentation in your mind or in front of a mirror. Imagine yourself being there and think about how you will start off, move around and deliver the whole thing.

When you practice with a group of colleagues or friends, do it as though they were the audience, and ask them to give you feedback on how well you did the following;

- Set the scene;
- Established good rapport;
- Covered the subject;
- Used your slides;
- Handled questions;
- Closed.

WORKSHEET

Every business should work in a structured way to maximise sales opportunity. This will obviously vary depending on what you sell.

The best process is always the one that's as simply as possible, and these questions will help you to see how the Navigator sales process can be applied to your business.

- How do you decide an opportunity is worth pursuing?
- How do you qualify prospects?
- Do you have a checklist or scoring system to identify the best fit?
- How do you work an opportunity when you get one?
- What's the process from initial contact to contract?
- How long does a typical sale take?
- How can the process be improved?

SALES PERFORMANCE

These questions will help you to get a sense of reality on your performance and identify what you need to do to achieve the results you are aiming for.

- How has your business grown in the last 12 months?
- How does this compare with previous periods?
- What does your current sales forecast look like?
- How often do you review it?
- Do you have a sales team?
- How well do they perform?
- Have they had training or skills development?
- Where do they need help?
- What are the problem areas to be addressed?
- Where can improvements be made?

SERVICE

This section does a similar thing for customer service as the previous one on sales performance. It's designed to identify issues and provide focus on what needs to change.

- What customer support do you provide?
- What are your goals and key measures of success?
- How often do you measure performance?
- How often do you ask your clients what they think of your service?
- What do you do with this information?
- Where can improvements be made?

INNOVATION

A key driver of competitive advantage is the ability to outperform your competitors. You can do this through product and service innovation.

- What's your product or service vision?
- What's your development roadmap?
- Who manages it?
- What are the key drivers of innovation?
- How do you generate and capture ideas?
- How do you incorporate the voice of the buyer?
- How well does this work?
- Where can you improve?

ABOUT ME

I'm a communication specialist, business coach and mentor and I help people create and deliver messages that are clear, concise and compelling.

After graduating in 1975 I worked in the Information Technology industry across Europe, India and North America. I've worked with Hewlett Packard, IBM, SAP and Microsoft and many start-ups who defined new market sectors.

It's been a lot of fun and hard work and during that time I've learned a lot. I've sold mainframes and minicomputers and witnessed the explosion of software application packages.

I've also lived through the total frenzy of the dot-com era where the start-up I worked for was at one stage valued at $40 billion, making it more valuable than General Motors. The truly mazing thing was that it had sales of $300 million and it never did make a profit!

Those were mad and crazy days, but I learned some very valuable lessons that I've applied to my thinking.

During recent years I've worked with fast growth companies, start-ups, spin-outs and established businesses in many different industry sectors.

It gives me such a buzz to work with people who are so enthusiastic and driven by their ideas. Often money is not their primary motivation, just a burning desire to create something different they can be really proud of.

I have an Honours degree in Economics and Social Psychology from Loughborough University and I live in Malvern, Worcestershire. For fun I play tennis and walk in wild places to take photographs. I'm also a lifelong lover of Welsh Rugby, a passion thankfully shared by my family!